Praise for *Troubled Minds*

"In *Troubled Minds* Amy Simpson opens the door into the hidden struggles of those caring for a mentally ill loved one. Between descriptions of her own real-life experiences she eloquently presents information that every Christian should have on how to recognize and appropriately respond to those living with mental illness. This book will prompt you (and your church) to action among a suffering people."

MATTHEW S. STANFORD, professor of psychology and neuroscience, Baylor University, and author, *Grace for the Afflicted*

"Having written about my own family's experience with mental illness, I know what it must have cost for Amy Simpson to root her highly informative book in her family's heartbreaking, yet hopeful story. Because of stigma and ignorance, far too many of us live with the pain of mental illness in silence and without compassionate support from our Christian communities. *Troubled Minds* has the potential to help free us from that quiet loneliness and bring our churches into fuller communion with those who suffer. I highly recommend it."

CHRISTINE A. SCHELLER, news and religion editor, UrbanFaith

"Amy Simpson gives deep insight into the pain of mental illness for those affected and those who love them. She makes puzzling concepts understandable, and she faces head-on the troubling questions raised by mental illness for people of faith. While I was reading the book, a homeless woman struggling with mental illness came to our church. Because of what I'd read, I interacted with her more patiently and effectively. I count this a must-read for pastors and church leaders."

KAREN MILLER, LCSW, executive pastor, Church of the Resurrection, Wheaton, Illinois

TROUBLED MINDS

MENTAL ILLNESS AND THE CHURCH'S MISSION

AMY SIMPSON

IVP Books

An imprint of InterVarsity Press
Downers Grove, Illinois

InterVarsity Press
P.O. Box 1400, Downers Grove, IL 60515-1426
World Wide Web: www.ivpress.com
Email: email@ivpress.com

InterVarsity Press® is the book-publishing division of InterVarsity Christian Fellowship/USA®, a movement of students and faculty active on campus at hundreds of universities, colleges and schools of nursing in the United States of America, and a member movement of the International Fellowship of Evangelical Students. For information about local and regional activities, write Public Relations Dept., InterVarsity Christian Fellowship/USA, 6400 Schroeder Rd., P.O. Box 7895, Madison, WI 53707-7895, or visit the IVCF website at <www.intervarsity.org>.

Unless otherwise indicated, all Scripture quotations are taken from the Holy Bible, New Living Translation, copyright ©1996, 2004. Used by permission of Tyndale House Publishers, Inc., Wheaton, Illinois 60189. All rights reserved.

All sidebar survey data comes from Leadership Journal survey on mental illness in churches, 2010. Used with permission from Leadership Journal/Christianity Today.

While all stories in this book are true, some names and identifying information in this book have been changed to protect the privacy of the individuals involved.

Cover design by Cindy Kiple
Interior design by Beth Hagenberg
Images: striped composition: © Qweek/iStockphoto; young male: © Pleio/iStockphoto

ISBN 978-0-8308-4304-6

Printed in the United States of America ∞

Library of Congress Cataloging-in-Publication Data

Simpson, Amy.
   Troubled minds : mental illness and the church's mission / Amy Simpson.
      pages cm
   Includes bibliographical references.
   ISBN 978-0-8308-4304-6 (pbk. : alk. paper)
   1. Church work with the mentally ill. 2. Mental illness—Religious aspects—Christianity. I. Title.
BV4461.S56 2013
261.8'322--dc23

                                                                              2013001569

| P | 18 | 17 | 16 | 15 | 14 | 13 | 12 | 11 | 10 | 9 | 8 | 7 | 6 | 5 | | |
| Y | 28 | 27 | 26 | 25 | 24 | 23 | 22 | 21 | 20 | 19 | 18 | 17 | 16 | 15 |

To my mother,
whose courage and spirit have
endured through suffering;

to my father,
whose faithfulness inspires my own;

to Trevor,
whose love helped bring me
to a place where I could write this,
and who hounded me until I
did something about it;

to Scott, Cheryl and Kate,
whose character through suffering
has sharpened mine;

and to my children,
who inspire me to be a stronger, healthier mom.

With all thanks and gratitude to God,
who has never let go of me.

CONTENTS

FOREWORD

Our culture has become increasingly transparent. Self-disclosure is accepted, even expected, in many settings. Whether in churches or bars, support groups or Bible studies, classrooms or offices, people feel free to talk about fears and phobias, addictions and abuse, issues in their family of origin, issues in their marriage and the challenges of being single.

For more than thirty years I have worked with church leaders, collecting their wisdom and hard-won insights to be published in *Leadership Journal*. Pastors almost universally have told me that people in their churches are now openly revealing things they would have kept silent about a generation ago: struggles with drugs, alcohol, gambling, pornography, affairs, domestic violence, estranged sons and daughters.

But in this day of increased openness, one topic is still taboo.

Mental illness.

Just today I was with a pastor in New Jersey, and I asked him if he was aware of anyone in his congregation who was taking medications for a mental illness. His immediate response was, "You're kidding, right?"

At first I misunderstood his response. I thought he meant that he was not aware of anyone. But then he said, "Of course there are people on meds. Mostly for severe depression and anxiety, but also several for bipolar disorder."

"How open are they about their condition?" I asked.

"No one knows," he said. "They've each told me, but they wouldn't feel comfortable talking openly about this. Mental illness is still very hard to admit to, even in a relatively safe small group. I'm grateful that these folks have shared their secret with me, their pastor."

"Why do you think they told you?"

"For most of them, because they wondered if it was okay to take meds for this condition. They wondered if it was a spiritual problem that they should just pray away. My job was to tell them I would indeed pray for them, but that mental illness is a condition like any physical illness. And that means it needs to be treated in medically appropriate ways, and often that means medication."

Almost two years ago I started talking about this topic with Amy Simpson, my colleague at Christianity Today. We both had experienced mental illness in our families, and we began wondering at the silence about mental illness in our church culture. Why is it easier to request prayer for alcoholism or addiction to pornography than for panic attacks or bipolar disorder?

Amy agreed to write an article for *Leadership Journal* about her family's experience. As we discussed plans for that article, we wondered how pervasive mental illness was within the church, and how churches were responding to it.

So in partnership with *Leadership Journal,* Amy conducted a survey of five hundred churches to get a sense of the scope of the problem. The results were overwhelming. Almost every church leader who responded (98.4 percent) indicated they are aware of mental illnesses or disorders among people in their congregations. (More details of the survey findings are reported elsewhere in this book.) This is hardly surprising, since almost 25 percent of the adult population has experienced some form of mental illness requiring medication, from depression to borderline personality disorder to autism to bipolar disorder to schizophrenia to posttraumatic stress disorder to obsessive-compulsive disorder to panic disorder.

If these church leaders are representative, nearly every church includes people with mental illness in its congregation.

But very few are confident in knowing how to respond. Mental illness, after all, is still a hard topic to talk about.

As Amy points out, even as we're enthusiastically delivering meals to people suffering physically, we are largely ignoring the afflictions of a quarter of our adult population who are suffering mentally. That's about equal to the total percentage of people diagnosed with cancer each year, those living with heart disease, people infected with HIV and AIDS, and those afflicted with diabetes— combined! No wonder several people Amy talked with called mental illness the "no-casserole illness."

This book is going to help change that! And I'm glad that you are reading it. Together we will be better prepared to respond compassionately and well to those with mental illness, and just as important, to family members and all the others who are affected by their condition. Thank you for helping to transform this taboo topic into another sphere into which we bring the love of God and the transforming power of the gospel.

Marshall Shelley
Editor-in-Chief, Leadership Journal

ACKNOWLEDGMENTS

I didn't know I could write this book. In fact, until a couple of years ago, I couldn't have done it. And when I started writing, I didn't know what I was in for. Growing up in the shadow of mental illness is a confusing and painful experience, and like many people, I developed emotional armor that protected me as I grew and helped me get along in the world. Talking (and writing) openly about mental illness and about some of my experiences has required me to shed many pieces of that armor. I had to battle my self-protective instincts and break my near-silence about my experience. This was a serious challenge—and a healing one.

It has taken me a long time and a lot of work to grow to a place where I can lower my defenses to this level and spend months thinking, talking and writing about a topic that hits so close to home. I want to give all glory to God and express thanks to my husband and to the professional counselors, friends and family who have walked this journey with me.

I extend a special thank-you to my mother, who generously allowed me to tell a bit of her story—far more painful than my own—in the hope that it will help many others. I also want to thank my father, my brother, Scott, and my sisters, Cheryl and Kate. They were open with me about their own experiences, and I'm grateful to them for their support as I've worked on what they could have perceived as a project airing our family's dirty laundry.

Writing this book has produced in me a fresh respect and affection for Mom, Dad and my siblings.

I met many wonderful people along this journey, and I thank everyone who shared a story of their struggle with mental illness or their efforts to help people they love. Thank you, Monica, Kevin, Marlena, Angie and all the others. And thank you, David Weiss, for letting me quote some material from your blog.

Thanks to the counseling professionals and pastors who took time to answer my questions and share their stories of ministry to hurting people.

Finally, I was encouraged by the ministries of people who are leading grassroots support groups in their churches. Cindy Hannan, Bob Mills, Jane and Fred Pramann, Elaine Tse and David Zucker—thank you for your generous spirits and for serving your brothers and sisters in the name of Christ. I hope this book inspires many more people to your kind of service.

INTRODUCTION

Y ou're writing a book about ministry to people with mental illness?"

"Yes, I am."

"Thank you so much for writing on this topic. The church really needs a book like that. . . . Can I tell you my own story?"

As I wrote this book, I had countless conversations like this. Nearly everyone I spoke with about the project had a story to share about their journey through mental illness or their walk alongside a loved one who suffered short-term or lifelong emotional or cognitive anguish.

There was the gentle woman who told me her husband has suffered with early-onset dementia for decades, turning their marriage into a long test of her faithfulness and self-sacrifice in caring for him. The friend who told me his easygoing demeanor masks an internal storm of anxiety and adrenaline surges he must control with medication. The man whose depression, untreated for years because of his church's condemnation, brought him to a point where he couldn't get out of bed and had to "risk God's rejection" by seeking treatment. Another man who had spent twenty-five years aching to relieve the anguish of his wife's depression. A father who had lost his twenty-something son to suicide after more than a decade of living with bipolar disorder. A woman who struggles to raise her children in the shadow of her parents' disorders. Parents of children debilitated by illness. People whose childhoods were disrupted by their ill parents' inability to give them the stable, loving homes they needed. Coworkers, friends, casual acquaintances. Strangers who contacted me after they read a magazine article I wrote. My own family, for whom this book served as a catalyst for healing conversations we had not yet had. People who are getting by with a gritty mix of vulnerability and fortitude, despair and hope, fear and faith. All shared with me stories they had kept mostly secret, some of them for decades.

Why? Because I've also suffered in the shadow of mental illness, and I was finally talking about it. Because what hurting people need, perhaps most of all, is to know that they are not alone, that someone else will hear their story and will love them just as much after they tell it. They need to know that their pain does not mean God has turned his back on them.

The suffering of mental illness, whether for the afflicted or for their families, is typically marked by isolation. When people desperately need to experience the love and empathy of their fellow human beings and to know that their Creator has not abandoned them, many reach out and are shocked to touch the church's painfully cold shoulder. Others fear the church's rejection enough to hide their struggles and not risk exposure at all.

Throughout the writing process, I've been encouraged to hear from many people about their experiences. It's uplifting for me to feel the support of others who have walked a similar road. It's invaluable to receive some confirmation that my writing project will connect with the experiences of many others. And it is heartbreaking reinforcement that the church needs this book.

Most people don't spend much time thinking about mental illness. Some have a vague sense that such illness is mostly confined to some kind of "institute" on the edge of town, where a doctor with a German accent analyzes the dreams of straitjacketed "crazy" people in padded rooms. Some assume that mental illness exists purely in the spiritual realm, believing it is a symptom of demon possession or weak faith. Others are confronted with the feral glances and paranoid mutterings of people on the street and quickly turn away, feeling helpless to make a difference and momentarily wondering whether anything can be done to help such people. They fear the behavior and afflictions of people they don't understand, so they dismiss mental illness as something that probably won't touch them.

Most people don't think about the mental health of their neighbors and friends, and people sitting next to them at church on Sunday morning. But the truth is, mental illness is everywhere. The statistics tell us that virtually everyone has been affected by it to some degree—some through their own illness and more of us through the challenge of relating to someone with a disorder.

Our society is growing dramatically in its acceptance of mental illness and its openness to discuss mental health publicly. Each year, the US Congress sanctions Mental Illness Awareness Week in October and Mental Health Month in May. In the news, we hear from a small but growing stream of celebrities who are willing to alter their public images with confessions of their own struggles with mental illness, in the name of making it easier for other people to get the help they need. Lawmakers and insurance companies are removing the discriminatory practices that have left so many people in the no man's land of insurance coverage with no diagnosis, no access to the care they need for treatable conditions and no hope of financial stability. Even Hollywood is treating mental illness with more accuracy and sensitivity.

Should the church be the last holdout in this movement toward grace? Should we be the ones clinging to old, fear-based beliefs that keep us convinced that people with mental illness should be isolated, shamed and silent—that their burdens are too great for the church to bear, their diagnoses too dire for the hope of Christ?

The church can and should be at the forefront of this move

toward loving acceptance and open support for those with mental illness. In the words of the apostle Paul, "God has put the body together such that extra honor and care are given to those parts that have less dignity. This makes for harmony among the members, so that all the members care for each other. If one part suffers, all the parts suffer with it, and if one part is honored, all the parts are glad" (1 Cor 12:24-26). Does this passage describe your church's approach to those among you who "have less dignity," those who are suffering?

The church can make a difference. The darkness is deep enough that even a tiny light can help someone find the way out. I spoke with one man who was hospitalized during an episode of severe depression as a young man. He said,

> I was sitting in the hospital and praying that someone would visit me. A few minutes after that, Dad showed up, and he had the pastor of our church with him. I was terrified of what he thought of me. Was he going to just pray with me? Was he going to lay his hands on me and make me happy? I had never really talked to him that much; I always just listened to him in church. The pastor told me that he and the church were praying, and I said, "What? You mean they are praying for me?"
>
> He said yes. And my father was nodding his head. Somehow the stigma came right out. I was going to say, "Please don't do that," and was getting ready to cry and beg them not to tell anyone. Then I looked over at another patient, my suite-mate on the ward, who was sitting in the corner ranting and raving to some imaginary person. It hit me: I have more than he does! I have a church praying for me!

If you're intrigued, hopeful, intimidated or overwhelmed, read on. You'll read about my family's experience in navigating the ongoing challenge of serious mental illness. You might be shocked to learn how common mental illness is. You'll hear from many people who can't afford not to think about mental illness, and you'll begin to understand something about the hardships they face. I hope you'll be grieved to read about the experiences of people both outside and inside the church. You'll read stories of people just like the ones in your own church, and you'll learn how you can help them. And you'll have the opportunity to consider why such ministry matters to God.

This is not a clinical work or an academic tome. It's not a gripe session or a tirade against the church. It's a book that the church needs because of both its practicality and its stories. It's filled with personal stories of those affected by mental illness, as well as helpful information about mental illness and how it is treated in the church.

The church allows people to suffer because we don't understand what they need and how to help them. We have taken our cue from the world around us and ignored, marginalized and laughed at the mentally ill or simply sent them to the professionals and washed our hands of them. This book will help you understand the prevalence of mental illness and the suffering it causes. But more important, it will help you understand the secondary suffering of the mentally ill within the church because of the church's response to them.

I recognize that each person's experiences and perspectives are unique, and my experiences and insights don't reflect the totality of experience with mental illness in the church. In this book I've attempted to capture a general sense of many people's reality, along with sharing my family's experience, to offer some insight into the challenge of ministry to people with mental illness. I hope you'll find that the pages of this book are filled with honesty and yet overflow with grace for both those directly affected by mental illness and those called to help suffering people in the context of the church.

In this book, you'll also find a heavy dose of hope. This hope is not based in what the church can do or in the efforts of a few committed and hard-working individuals. It is based in the power and grace of Christ, who is always with us and who will not allow anything to separate us from his love. "Neither death nor life, neither angels nor demons, neither our fears for today nor our worries about tomorrow—not even the powers of hell can separate us from God's love" (Rom 8:38).

This hope is also based in the comfort of God's constant presence with us, even when we can't feel him and when trouble threatens to overwhelm us. As Paul wrote,

> We are pressed on every side by troubles, but we are not crushed. We are perplexed, but not driven to despair. We are hunted down, but never abandoned by God. We get knocked down, but we are not destroyed. Through suffering, our bodies continue to share in the death of Jesus so that the life of Jesus may also be seen in our bodies. (2 Cor 4:8-10)

Our hope is rooted in our knowledge that something much better is on its way. For no matter how deep the darkness, how painful life can be in this decaying world, as children of God we can always look forward to the day when "our bodies are buried in brokenness, but they will be raised in glory. They are buried in weakness, but they will be raised in strength" (1 Cor 15:43).

1

A FAMILY STORY

My story begins as many do—quietly, and with only a hint of what is coming.

I grew up in the Midwest, one of four kids in a loving family. Dad was a pastor for ten years, serving two small rural churches. Mom was a homemaker. Our family loved to go camping, and all of my best memories of family life have the six of us crammed into a pop-up camper, swimming in a lake somewhere or sweating together with the wind thrashing our hair, three in the front and three in the back of our sedan.

My parents have adventurous spirits and great passion for serving Jesus. Before I was born, they decided to become missionaries to Africa and worked their way through the process of approval and fundraising in their pursuit of this plan. When I was a toddler, Mom and Dad packed all our belongings in barrels for shipment overseas and moved the family to Lausanne, Switzerland. We spent a year there while my parents did intensive study of the French language.

The plan was to go to Africa after that year and to join the missionary work underway in what was then Zaire. When the time came, however, political tensions prevented our going. We went back to the United States, and Dad decided to pursue pastoral ministry instead. I've often wondered what our lives would have been like if I had grown up in Africa. And I've wondered what would have happened if the life that unfolded had instead unfolded in a missionary outpost half the world away.

My mom is a gentle person, creative, funny, resourceful and very smart. She always encouraged my creative development, indulged my love for reading, taught me to clean the house like I meant it, sparked my love of a good pun and showed me how to get organized. Mom is also the person who led me to faith in Christ when I was only four years old.

Yet there's more to our story. Mom has suffered tremendously and has been the source of much of my own suffering. Ours is a very complicated relationship—as all her relationships are. While I didn't know enough to question the normalcy of our family life when I was a child, I knew something was wrong. This undefined knowledge nagged at my family as we did our best to ignore it. As it became harder to ignore, we started looking for help—and came up short. When I was a teenager, on the day I waited at school for someone to pick me up and no one came, it became obvious.

My brother, who had stopped at home on a break between college classes, had found Mom in the kitchen, completely unable to function. She went to the hospital. When I called home from a pay phone to find out when someone would pick me up from school, a neighbor answered and said Mom had had "a stroke or something." I walked the two miles home from school, praying and worrying about what this "stroke or something" would mean. Was she going to be okay? Was she dying? Would I lose my mom? Would our family be the same?

It wouldn't be the same. Life changed after that. And yes, I did lose my mom—over and over again.

It was no stroke that had indelibly altered Mom and our family. That was the day she had her first full-on, debilitating, confusing, terrifying, mind-bending, truth-twisting, hospital-worthy psychotic break. And it was a long time before I understood what had happened.

My family hiccupped through this episode but kept going; when we got Mom back, we did our best to live as if what had happened was no big deal. Mom started seeing a Christian counselor and said she was struggling with depression. Meanwhile, she moved around the house like a zombie, her functioning almost completely suppressed by the powerful antipsychotics she got at the hospital. My younger sister and I picked up the slack and tiptoed around Mom as if she were a sleeping ghost. When she was hospitalized again (and again and again) we adopted Unspoken Rules 1, 2 and 3 by consensus: Don't talk about it. Everything is fine. No one outside this family will understand.

A Public Crisis

When I was fifteen, Mom picked me up at school to take me to a dental appointment. I could tell immediately that she wasn't functioning normally; I recognized warning signs that she was headed for another "episode." She drove nervously, as if struggling to be fully aware of her surroundings, or perhaps imagining surroundings that weren't there. She was silent except when I forced conversation, and when she did speak, her speech was slow and seemed to require deliberation. Her interaction with me was indirect and stiff, as if she were not fully aware that I was there. She seemed to be fading, as if half of her had already shrunk into an unknown place and the other half was not sure whether to follow or to maintain its grip on the reality of a daughter and a trip to the dentist.

I remember thanking God that I could legally take over driving if I needed to and asking Mom if she had taken her medication that day. Her answer was not straightforward, but it was clear she was not fully medicated and stable. So, with one part of my brain,

I prayed for a safe trip to the dentist. With another part, I employed a technique used by many people who feel powerless in the face of an unnamed threat: I soothed myself by acting as if nothing were wrong.

We did make our way safely to the dental office, and we sat down to wait. When my name was called, I left my mother in the waiting room and went back for my appointment. I also stepped out of my anxiety about her for the moment, as I did when I was away from her—part of my strategy for coping with a devastating stress I didn't understand.

After half an hour or so with the dentist, I returned to the waiting room and approached my mom, who didn't look at me. "Mom, it's time to go," I said. "I'm finished." No response of any kind. Suddenly I realized my instincts had been right, and my earlier fear was realized: something indeed was wrong with Mom . . . again. And it was up to me to help her. I touched her arm and gently tried to shake her back to awareness, with no results. She was rigidly catatonic, immovable, staring into space and clutching her purse in her lap with clenched hands—in a waiting room full of strangers.

After a couple of quiet attempts to rouse her, I began to attract attention. People sat and stared at me, wide-eyed, as I tried to get her to respond. *If I could just get her to the car,* I thought, *I could take her home or to the hospital or wherever. I have to get her out of here.* But when she wouldn't move or even respond to me, I realized I wouldn't be able to get her to the car; I would have to call Dad at work for help.

With everyone in the room continuing to stare, I walked over to the reception desk and asked the woman behind the counter—who was also staring—if I could use the phone. "No, there's a pay phone around the corner." When I explained that I needed to call my dad for help, I didn't have change for the phone, and it would be a local call, she still refused and pointed to the pay phone. So I went back to my mom and wrestled with her rigid arms, pulling them aside enough to get into her purse and get the quarter I needed for the phone. I went back to the receptionist to ask if she could keep an eye on my mom while I went to use the pay phone. She shrank back in horror and asked, "Is she dangerous?"

After assuring the receptionist that my absolutely motionless mother was not about to attack her, I called my dad and then returned to sit next to Mom and wait for him to arrive. The receptionist and the people in the waiting room took turns staring at her, glancing at me and studying the floor. And not one person asked me—a completely rational and nonthreatening fifteen-year-old kid—if I needed help.

While Dad was on his way, one of the dentists became aware of what was happening and did what she could to help get Mom to the car. Dad and I took her to the hospital for another of her psychiatric stays and restabilization on medication. After she had received some medication and was waiting for a more intensive evaluation and admission, she became somewhat responsive. I could tell she was terrified of something, and I talked with her, trying to help her with words of reassurance and trying to understand why she was scared. While still not speaking, she began responding to me through hand gestures, nods and shakes of her head. Someone was trying to hurt her, she thought. Someone was trying to hurt us all.

What she was communicating didn't make sense, but I tried to understand it anyway. I really wanted to help her, but I didn't understand the nature of psychosis—let alone that my mom was psychotic and our communication was badly distorted. I hoped that by communicating with her and soothing her fears, I could "fix" her. As she gestured to me and I responded gently, tears rolled freely down her face, and my heart broke. I kept telling her she was going to be okay; she kept shaking her head and crying. Then they admitted her and took her away, and I went home with Dad and back to "regular" life. I never talked to anyone about what I had experienced.

Life Goes On

Although I didn't know this at the time of the incident in the dental office, my mother has schizophrenia, a chronic, seriously disruptive and potentially devastating biologically and environmentally based mental illness. As often happens with people who have schizophrenia, at that time she had not been faithfully taking her antipsychotic drugs and had lost touch with reality. She would be stabilized in the hospital and sent home—once again to make her way in a world that despised and misunderstood mental illness, alongside a family who loved her but couldn't make her better.

During those high school years and the following decades, Mom's illness profoundly affected our family life. My older sister went to college nearby and spent a lot of herself trying to make sure my younger sister and I were okay—but we never talked about what was wrong with Mom. We were all trying to cope, and we lacked the language and strength to drag it out into the open.

So my younger sister and I hung laundry out on a clothesline in the middle of the city because Mom believed our clothes dryer was possessed by demons. We watched Mom wander the house in a drugged-up haze, sewed our own clothes, cooked for the family, went camping by ourselves, visited Mom in the hospital and kept an eye on her handwriting—because she wrote with her left hand when her symptoms were stronger. I tucked her in at night with my favorite childhood stuffed animal and constantly watched for signs that the cycle of breakdown and hospitalization was starting again.

Mom made her way dreamily through my high school graduation. When it came time for me to select a college, I was determined to put some distance between me and my home. I struggled and stressed over all the information I'd gathered and couldn't make a decision. When my parents offered to help, I realized I was so independent, it hadn't even occurred to me to ask them to participate in the decision.

At college, I opened my campus mailbox to "letters" from Mom—actually colored pictures from coloring books. And when she and Dad came to my college graduation, my husband and I woke the next morning to find her catatonic on the floor in our apartment. The journey hasn't ended with independent adulthood. Every year has brought its own adventure and every visit a new kind of heartbreak. I have lost sleep before visits to my parents' house, wondering what we would find when we arrived. I have wistfully met my friends' moms at their baby showers, wondering what it would be like to have a relationship like that. I have hungered for older women to serve as mentors to me, unsure how to find what I'm longing for. I have cringed my way through Mother's Day sermons and through movies that portray people with schizophrenia as raging monsters, subhuman sources of amusement or sage prophets. I have lived in fear of other people finding out the truth about my family and rejecting me, of hearing that my mom had fallen victim to something horrible, of losing my own mental stability.

Several years ago, when Mom was not properly medicated, she began to believe she was receiving hidden meanings behind what she heard at church. She eventually believed these spiritual delusions were true and sought more insights through studying the occult. After a while, she rejected her Christian beliefs and fully embraced occult practices and fellowship. Our family was heartbroken. We agonized our way through many conversations with her about the truth she had spent her life believing, but she was firmly committed to her new way of life. She was also irrational and confused, and we knew she was not medicated as she should have been. But we could not force her to get the treatment she needed.

One day I received a call at work, telling me Mom had disap-
peared. She had left home with no indication of where she was
going, and no one we knew had heard from her. I agonized and
tried to help my sister—who lives close to my parents—look for
her. Months later when, by God's grace, we found her living in a
homeless shelter, my sister tried to coax her out of the shelter,
whose staff had already coaxed her off the streets. She was so psychotic, she barely recognized my sister and had almost no awareness
of her family.

Working with the shelter staff, we were able to get her into a
hospital program and get her back on the proper medication, but
the damage had been done. A few months later she was arrested for
a crime she had been accused of while living in shelters, and eventually she was convicted of a felony and sentenced to prison.

One of the worst days of my life was the day I saw Mom's mug shot
on the website for the state penitentiary. One of the hardest things I've
done is take my children to visit their grandma in a state hospital,
where she was incarcerated for ten months after she was released
from prison. I've explained to my children that Grandma loves them
but her brain doesn't work the way ours do, so sometimes she says
and does unexpected things because she is sick and her medication
doesn't always work right. At times I've kept my children far away
from her. And all along I've tried to understand who Mom is apart
from schizophrenia, partly so I can understand and accept who I
am—especially the parts of me that are so much like her.

And so our family's journey continues—a winding, rocky and
stumbling journey with an illness that in many ways has defined us
and that has shocked us again and again with its ugliness as it has
developed in stages over time.

The Church

Throughout this journey, we have been in the church. The church
has been, for the most part, either oblivious or a silent observer,

solidly placed in the part of our lives where people don't understand and where we pretend everything is fine.

In my years since the lonely incident in the dental office, I've often thought back to it as a reference point for attitudes toward the mentally ill and their families. The way people in that waiting room responded to my family's public crisis is the way I've seen people in general—including in the church—respond to serious mental illness. To them, my mother was to be feared and I was somehow infected by my association with her. The people around me felt helpless and fearful, and they did nothing to help.

I think we can do better. I think we can be more like the church we were made to be.

The church is the body of Christ—the physical manifestation of Jesus' presence on earth. "It is made full and complete by Christ, who fills all things everywhere with himself" (Eph 1:23). We play host to the Holy Spirit of God, represent and reflect the God of the universe to the world around us and represent that same God to each other. We are the bride of Christ, beautiful and radiant and waiting eagerly for that walk down the aisle to eternity.

We are also deeply wounded and flawed. We are imperfect as a body and imperfect as individual bodies. We are wrecked by sin and its consequences, fully as wrecked and disfigured as those around us. No one is left untouched by life in a world like ours, where

> all creation is waiting eagerly for that future day when God will reveal who his children really are. Against its will, all creation was subjected to God's curse. But with eager hope, the creation looks forward to the day when it will join God's children in glorious freedom from death and decay. For we know that all creation has been groaning as in the pains of childbirth right up to the present time. And we believers also

groan, even though we have the Holy Spirit within us as a foretaste of future glory, for we long for our bodies to be released from sin and suffering. We, too, wait with eager hope for the day when God will give us our full rights as his adopted children, including the new bodies he has promised us. (Rom 8:19-23)

Yes, someday God will recreate our bodies, and all our suffering will end. This includes the suffering of our minds when our brains are sick or malfunctioning. For centuries, the church has been inspired by this promise: "We are citizens of heaven, where the Lord Jesus Christ lives. And we are eagerly waiting for him to return as our Savior. He will take our weak mortal bodies and change them into glorious bodies like his own, using the same power with which he will bring everything under his control" (Phil 3:20-21). We hold to this promise—cling to it desperately at times—and look forward to a glorious and awakened life in a world we can't even imagine.

Unfortunately, we grow impatient and lose sight of the eternal perspective the Holy Spirit nurtures within us. As the Lord and his glorious grace grow strangely dim in our minds, we focus more and more on the here and now. We feel our aches and pains, anxieties and restlessness, and we think, *This is not the way life is supposed to be.* And we're right. But life as it should be is outside our grasp in this world. As we pursue the life we think we should have, we begin to insist that health and happiness are normal and the most tangible indicators of God's favor—to which we believe we're entitled. We see the suffering of others and wonder why they have lost favor with God.

We are so uncomfortable with being forgiven and called and yet weak and suffering, we turn away from the suffering and weakness in our midst. We reject them in the name of our claim on a world we don't yet live in. We try to amputate those parts of the body of Christ that exhibit the most suffering. We don't want to look at them, because they remind us of what we're trying to forget—the truth about every single one of us.

As the body of Christ and an instrument of God's communication with the world, the church must "do to others as you would like them to do to you" (Lk 6:31). We are called to be a place where "it doesn't matter if you are a Jew or a Gentile, circumcised or uncircumcised, barbaric, uncivilized, slave, or free. Christ is all that matters, and he lives in all of us" (Col 3:11). A place where we are "agreeing wholeheartedly with each other, loving one another, and working together with one mind and purpose" (Phil 2:2).

Paul wrote this of the church's mission:

> Since God chose you to be the holy people he loves, you must clothe yourselves with tenderhearted mercy, kindness, humility, gentleness, and patience. Make allowance for each other's faults, and forgive anyone who offends you. Remember, the Lord forgave you, so you must forgive others. Above all, clothe yourselves with love, which binds us all together in perfect harmony. And let the peace that comes from Christ rule in your hearts. For as members of one body you are called to live in peace. And always be thankful.
>
> Let the message about Christ, in all its richness, fill your lives. Teach and counsel each other with all the wisdom he gives. Sing psalms and hymns and spiritual songs to God with thankful hearts. And whatever you do or say, do it as a representative of the Lord Jesus, giving thanks through him to God the Father. (Col 3:12-17)

This is what the church is created to do. This is our mission statement. Ours is supposed to be a community where the hurting, broken and sin-scarred find rest and redemption. Where everyone present owns up to being a hurting, broken and sin-scarred individual, rescued from the ultimate death, the ultimate suffering—which we deserve—by the grace of God. Where that same grace causes us to reach outside ourselves and, through the Holy Spirit's power, love one another.

This is the church as it should be.

Sadly, we often fall short of what we should be. And we certainly fall short in accepting, reaching out to and loving people with mental illness and their families—who at times may be among the weakest and most acutely suffering people we know. We can do better; we've all seen the church act as a beacon of hope in a dark world—sometimes in spite of our bumbling efforts. We've all borne witness to the power of Christ to change a life, sometimes through the actions of his people. As we seek to become more like the community he created us to be, let's pause and try to understand the kind of suffering mental illness visits on so many individuals and families.

2

MENTAL ILLNESS
IS MAINSTREAM

For the first couple of decades of Mom's full-blown illness and my family's crisis, one of the greatest catalysts to our pain was the sense that we were alone. Because we suffered mostly silently, we didn't find other people who were suffering in the same way. And because those other suffering people were silent too, we all thought we were the only ones. Now I know better. We weren't even close to alone.

Most people are surprised to learn that mental illness is incredibly common. In fact, mental disorders are the number-one cause of disability in North America. According to the National Institute of Mental Health and other experts, about one in four adults—a little more than 25 percent of Americans ages eighteen and older—suffers from a diagnosable mental disorder in a given year.[1] Yes, one in four. That equates to around fifty million people in the United States. And that's only *in a given year*. Because many mental illnesses (like depressive episodes) are short-term and not chronic, a higher percentage of people are affected by a mental illness at some point in their lives.

Serious and chronic mental illness is less common but still

present among 6 percent of the population, or one in seventeen adults. That's almost twelve million people in the United States. Those mental illnesses considered "serious" are major depression, schizophrenia, bipolar disorder, obsessive-compulsive disorder (OCD), panic disorder, posttraumatic stress disorder (PTSD) and borderline personality disorder.[2]

Other mental illnesses, while not as serious as those called clinically "serious" by psychiatrists, still must be taken seriously. The National Alliance on Mental Illness (NAMI) defines mental illnesses as "medical conditions that disrupt a person's thinking, feeling, mood, ability to relate to others and daily functioning" and "often result in a diminished capacity for coping with the ordinary demands of life."[3] All mental illness, by definition, impairs a person's basic functioning and disrupts the kind of social connections God created us to enjoy (see Gen 2:18-23; Col 3:12-15; 1 Jn 4:7-12).

Antipsychotics are now the top-selling class of drugs in the United States. This is because of their growing use not only to treat serious psychotic disorders but also to address a broader array of problems.[4] These drugs have powerful side effects, which contributes to the reluctance of people who need them to take them consistently. These side effects themselves can impair a person's functioning as powerfully as an illness can.

What about those under the age of eighteen? Many people think of mental illness as an adult problem because such illnesses in children are not as well documented and well known as they are in adults. People hesitate to diagnose—and thereby label—children, who are still forming and who may "grow out of" a mental illness. Perhaps another reason is that, because our bodies begin to break down as we age, we tend to associate illness in general with adulthood. And we find it especially tragic when people in the "prime of life" go through serious suffering.

But the nature of much mental illness makes it different from most other disabling disease. The National Institute of Mental Health calls mental disorders "the chronic diseases of the young." Many of these disorders begin early in life. According to one of the institute's press releases,

> Half of all lifetime cases begin by age 14; three quarters have begun by age 24. . . . For example, anxiety disorders often begin in late childhood, mood disorders in late adolescence, and substance abuse in the early 20s. Unlike heart disease or most cancers, young people with mental disorders suffer disability when they are in the prime of life, when they would normally be the most productive.[5]

According to the US Surgeon General, every year an estimated 20 percent of children in the United States are at least mildly impaired by some type of diagnosable mental illness. And about 5 to 9 percent of children ages nine to seventeen have a "serious emotional disturbance."[6] That's between three and seven million children in serious trouble—and millions of families in crisis.

Nearly everyone is touched by mental illness—directly or indirectly—at some point. From the millions of people with diagnosable mental illness, the suffering extends to parents, children, grandparents, siblings, aunts, uncles, friends, coworkers, neighbors and church members. If your church is typical of the US population, on any given Sunday one in four adults and one in five children sitting around you are suffering from a mental illness. Many of them are under the influence of powerful antipsychotic drugs and their side effects.

The Church's Response to Disease

Against the backdrop of knowledge about various types of mental illness and their frequency, consider the statistics for a few other types of serious illness.

Heart disease. Heart disease is a serious problem. In the United States, it is responsible for 26 percent of deaths, with approximately 0.2 percent of the population dying from heart disease every year.[7] According to the Centers for Disease Control and Prevention, 11.5 percent of adults in the United States have some kind of heart disease.[8]

Cancer. Cancer strikes more than 1.5 million people, with new diagnoses every year in the United States.[9] That means about 0.5 percent of the population is diagnosed with cancer annually. This includes the entire population—all ages and races—and all forms of cancer.

HIV and AIDS. The Centers for Disease Control and Prevention estimates that approximately fifty thousand people are infected with HIV each year in the United States.[10] That's about 0.01 percent of the population. An estimated thirty-five thousand (0.01 percent) per year develop AIDS and just over one million (3.7 percent) are living with AIDS.[11]

Diabetes. According to the American Diabetes Association, 25.8 million people—adults and children—in the United States are afflicted with diabetes. This is about 8 percent of the population. Among adults age twenty and older, 11 percent have diabetes, and about two million cases are diagnosed each year.[12]

These diseases are serious, life threatening and grief inducing. They provide clear evidence of humanity's great fall, with its consequences of decay and inevitable death. Everything we touch turns to dust, including these cursed bodies of ours. Because of genetic predispositions and lifestyle choices, we all participate in the suffering that is our lot as people living in the shadow of rebellion against the God of the universe. And sometimes, because we are drawn to our foolishness like a dog to its own vomit (Prov 26:11), we actually hasten death through our choices.

So, what does the church do in the face of these consequences of sin? We rightly minister to the victims of these diseases. Over recent decades, the church has grown more open in its acceptance of suffering people and in its willingness to suffer alongside them. We visit them in the hospital, raise money to fight their diseases and pay their bills. We bring them meals, drive them to appointments and babysit their kids. We pray for them in our services, ask them how they're feeling and accommodate them with special foods at our potlucks.

And as we're busy enthusiastically delivering meals to suffering people, we are largely ignoring the afflictions of 25 percent of our population. That's about equal to the total percentage of people diagnosed with cancer each year, those living with heart disease, those infected with HIV and AIDS and those afflicted with diabetes—combined. No wonder several people I talked with called mental illness the "no-casserole illness." In contrast to the care we provide for others, we have very little patience with those whose diseases happen to attack their minds. And many people suffer in silence.

A Brief Overview of Mental Illness

Given the prevalence of mental illness, it seems wise—no, critical—to understand the basic types of mental illness and how they affect people. The following are broad categories of disorders with general explanations. Please keep in mind that these categories and lists are not exhaustive, and descriptions do not include all possibilities.

As I write this, I'm holding a copy of the most recent edition of the *Diagnostic and Statistical Manual of Mental Disorders*, the authoritative and exhaustive reference manual for mental health professionals, which includes detailed explanations and definitions of mental disorders. It's 886 pages long, and it reflects an unfolding and inexact science that categorizes some illnesses with names like "Mental disorders due to a general medical condition not elsewhere classified." So, obviously, I will not be able to capture in a few pages all the detail and scope of known mental illnesses.

I've chosen to stick closely to the general categories used by the National Institute of Mental Health because they are broad enough to cover most illness and concise enough that they shouldn't overwhelm us with too much information.

Anxiety disorders. Frank was a forty-five-year-old father of three and a business executive, happily married and energized in his job. He had lived in his community for four years and was beginning to feel settled. His kids had great friends and were doing well in school. His oldest child was seventeen and looking forward to graduating from high school.

One day at work, Frank received a frantic call from his son, saying his mother (Frank's wife) was on her way to the hospital after being hit by a car and sustaining a severe head injury. Frank rushed to the hospital and remained there for three days until the doctors determined that her brain was no longer functioning and she would never come out of her coma. Frank and his kids made the torturous decision to "unplug" the machines and let their precious wife and mother pass away. He held his in her arms until well after she took her last breath.

It's been a year now since his wife's death. Although Frank remains a business executive, his three children are struggling in school for the first time. He has become socially withdrawn and is no longer doing things he used to enjoy. He doesn't sleep for more than four hours a night. He has recurring nightmares about holding his wife as she died and acknowledges the only reason he hasn't ended his life is because of his children's dependence on him. When they're all in college, he hopes he'll be able to leave this world because it no longer seems worthwhile for him to be here.

He knows he's depressed, but he's not interested in going to support groups or talking about the wife he lost. Support groups only increase his anxiety, sadness and anger. He avoids the topic of her death at all costs and hasn't opened the door to her closet since that last day of her stay at the hospital. He fears that his children will die and is convinced that it is up to him alone to keep them safe and alive. He has become hypervigilant to ensure their safety. His recurrent thoughts and reminders of his lost wife are debilitating.

Definition. Anxiety disorders, like some other types of mental illness, are defined by excess. A certain level of anxiety is normal for all of us, especially during times of stress. When a disorder is present, a person experiences so much anxiety that it consistently interferes with daily functioning—sometimes severely. The anxiety may or may not be tied to a specific source of fear, worry or stress.

Characteristics. People with anxiety disorders may feel the same symptoms of anxiety that we all experience: worry, stress, elevated heart rate, shortness of breath, sweating. They may experience these symptoms to an extreme degree or over prolonged periods. They may also express their anxiety in more disruptive ways, such as through obsessive thoughts, compulsive actions, flashbacks to traumatic events, sleeplessness, intense and paralyzing fear, or an overall sense of dread.

Prevalence. According to the National Institute of Mental Health, each year 18 percent of adults in the United States experience an anxiety disorder of some kind. Twenty-two percent of those disorders are classified as severe.[13] Anxiety disorders are among the most common form of mental illness.

Some specific anxiety disorders:

- agoraphobia
- generalized anxiety disorder (GAD)
- obsessive-compulsive disorder (OCD)
- panic disorder
- posttraumatic stress disorder (PTSD)
- social anxiety disorder
- a specific phobia

Family impact. Although Frank's entire family has walked through this tragedy together and each person is grieving, Frank has experienced this differently. His friendships have suffered. And his relationships with his kids are collapsing as his parenting presence is greatly diminished.

His constant mourning over the past year has not allowed the rest of the family to move forward or to have what they need from him. His children are suppressing their emotions to avoid rocking the boat, and the family has not moved back into a normal pattern of interacting with one another, because of the consistent intensity of his grief. The kids are starting to feel angry and act out at home and with their friends.

Without successful intervention, Frank will likely remain in a perpetual state of anxiety and depression over the loss of his wife, and he may lose his connection to his kids.

Attention-deficit/hyperactivity disorder (ADHD). Nine-year-old Jacob is having trouble making it through the school day without scoldings from several of his teachers. He constantly roams the classroom and requires redirection several times an hour to remain on task and engaged in the lesson at hand. His peers complain that he steals their school supplies and picks on them. Jacob loves to make other students laugh and often makes noises and jokes in the middle of class to get attention from his peers. On the playground, he frequently fights with peers during game time because he refuses to follow the rules and acts very bossy. Because of these social problems, Jacob is increasingly negative and depressed, saying, "I'm an idiot. I hate myself, and I wish I was dead."

Intellectually, Jacob is very bright. His cognitive abilities test well in the standardized tests given at school, but his schoolwork is poor and is rarely turned in or done correctly. He's failing all of his classes and may be retained during the next school year.

His parents see a lot of behavior problems at home as well. Neither his teachers nor his parents have been able to determine whether his disruptive behavior comes from a lack of impulse control or from defiance and manipulation. His teachers hope his parents will agree to him getting psycho-educational testing to determine whether he has ADHD.

Definition. Attention-deficit/hyperactivity disorder is most commonly diagnosed in children because symptoms usually begin before age seven. Attention problems and hyperactivity (not just one or the other) must be present for an ADHD diagnosis. This is a neurologically based disorder, the exact cause of which is still unknown. Scientists have uncovered evidence of genetic transmission, and environmental causes seem to play a part.

Characteristics. People with ADHD have trouble focusing their attention, sustaining focus and shifting focus from one thing to another. They may be easily distracted and may have a short attention span. They also exhibit hyperactivity (overactivity). Sufferers may have trouble controlling their impulses and behavior. While commonly diagnosed in childhood, ADHD can continue through adolescence and adulthood.

Prevalence. According to the National Institute of Mental Health, each year 4 percent of adults in the United States live with ADHD. Forty-one percent of those cases are classified as severe.[14] Nine percent of thirteen- to eighteen-year-olds will experience ADHD, and 1.8 percent of adolescents will experience a "severe" case.[15] Attention-deficit/hyperactivity disorder is much more common in males than in females, and it is one of the most common disorders in children.

Some specific expressions of ADHD:
There are three different types of ADHD, differentiated by which symptoms dominate:

- . predominantly hyperactive-impulsive
- predominantly inattentive
- combined hyperactive-impulsive and inattentive

Family impact. Jacob's parents have long noticed that he is more active and intense than his peers and friends. They have often used the phrase "boys will be boys" in reference to Jacob's rambunctious behavior. They grieve for him when they hear that he wishes he were dead and that he hates himself. They have read parenting books about "strong-willed" kids and about active boys, but they have not found anything that really works with Jacob.

Deep down, they suspect he may be a kid who could be diagnosed with ADHD, but they don't want him labeled and medicated. They are just about to go to another meeting at school, where they will be two of eleven people in a room discussing their concerns. This is scary and frustrating for them.

Autism spectrum disorders (ASD). Jane is a secondgrader in a class of twenty-five students. She is gentle and loves to read. She speaks brilliantly and has a particular fascination with clouds and weather. She appears to be socially awkward and doesn't have any reciprocal friendships. Her classmates play with her to be nice and inclusive—out of obligation. She never initiates conversations with her peers and rarely even talks to them. When a peer asks a question, she responds with a short, blunt answer. This is odd to her parents and teachers because she is so fluent in talking about science and the weather. When she's speaking, she doesn't make eye contact, even when prompted to. Jane apparently prefers to be alone at recess and loves skipping the lines on the playground in a dance-type fashion.

Definition. Autism spectrum disorders are a group of developmental disorders of the brain that fall along a spectrum of severity and symptoms. These disorders become apparent in childhood and seem to be caused by both genetic and environmental factors, especially during fetal development. They impair social functioning, communication and normal emotional responses. Most people with autism spectrum disorders are diagnosed before age eight.

Characteristics. People with ASD do not communicate with

others or express emotions the way most people do. They have social difficulties that go beyond mere shyness or awkwardness to actual impairment. The severity of the impairment depends on the specific disorder, with autism producing a much more severe impairment than its milder cousin, Asperger syndrome. People with ASD may make little eye contact, seem not to notice the presence or communication efforts of other people, have difficulty understanding social cues and use language in a limited way or in a way that only people who know that person well can understand. They may also engage in repetitive behaviors like moving fingers or arms in the same way over and over, walking in patterns or repeating words or phrases. In one sense, ASD is the opposite of ADHD: people with ASD tend to be overly focused and may focus obsessively on one thing for a long time. Symptoms usually begin in young childhood and may be present even in infancy.

Prevalence. According to the Centers for Disease Control and Prevention's Autism and Developmental Disabilities Monitoring (ADDM) Network, an estimated one in 110 (about 1 percent) of children in the United States have autism spectrum disorders.[16] Like ADHD, ASD is much more common (estimated at about four times more common) in males than in females.

Some specific autism spectrum disorders:

- Asperger's disorder (Asperger syndrome)

- autistic disorder

- childhood disintegrative disorder (CDD)

- Rett's disorder (Rett syndrome)

Family impact. Jane's parents have noticed that she acts differently than her older brothers and sisters. She has never been very affectionate or snuggly. For a while, they thought they were doing something wrong and their daughter didn't like them. Jane was very rigid in the way she played, and she didn't adjust well in times of transition in any context. She would often seem to be in her own little world.

When Jane began stating impressive statistics about weather and became a voracious reader, they found peace in thinking she was a quirky, introverted child who just connected better with adults. But they are becoming deeply concerned with her inability to connect with her peers.

Eating disorders. Betty is a thirty-five-year-old woman with an extremely thin build and thin hair, and her skin does not look healthy. Her husband divorced her last year to the relief of her friends and family, who found him mean and domineering. Betty was devastated by the divorce and convinced herself that he had left her because she wasn't pretty enough.

Since she was a teenager, Betty had been very concerned about her weight and her appearance. After the divorce, she spent more and more time—hours—in front of the mirror, combing her hair and looking at her body. She weighed herself more than twenty times a day and was constantly trying to hit the "perfect" weight. Unfortunately, that weight always moved lower and lower. Betty was eating approximately two hundred calories a day, often limiting herself to a leaf of lettuce and half a cup of water. She'd insist that was all she needed and would go about functioning normally throughout the day.

One day, she passed out, and a neighbor found her on the floor. She was taken to the emergency room and diagnosed with anorexia nervosa. Betty thought this was preposterous and dismissed the hospital staff's claims. She placated them with a commitment to eat, and they insisted that she eat her food in front of them. She refused and left the hospital against medical advice.

Betty's family and friends grow increasingly concerned for her and spend a lot of time checking on her and trying to convince her to eat. She's unable to see the reality of her situation, and the people who love her are starting to wonder how long she can keep living this way.

Definition. Eating disorders are just what they sound like: disorders that affect people's relationship with food. These disorders also affect body image and are marked by extreme behavior. These are not merely bad habits, occasional overindulgence or dieting. These are extreme disturbances to emotions, perceptions and behavior.

Eating disorders most frequently appear during adolescence or early adulthood, but they can develop during childhood or in adulthood. These illnesses can be life threatening without treatment. People with anorexia nervosa are eighteen times more likely to die early than people in the general population.[17] Eating disorders affect both men and women, although more women suffer from anorexia nervosa and bulimia nervosa. Men and women suffer roughly equally from binge-eating disorder.[18]

Characteristics. People with eating disorders go to extremes in their relationship to food, either undereating or overeating. Overeating is typically followed either by purging (vomiting, using laxatives, fasting or exercising excessively) or by weight gain and intense distress over the consequences of overeating, which may lead to more overeating. People with eating disorders are obsessed with food and possess distorted images of their bodies. In particular, people with anorexia nervosa truly see themselves as overweight, even when they are emaciated and literally starving to death. People with eating disorders commonly experience other mental illnesses as well, such as depression and anxiety disorders.

Prevalence. According to the National Institute of Mental Health, anorexia nervosa and bulimia nervosa each affect 0.6 percent of adults in the United States. Binge-eating disorder affects 2.8 percent over the course of a lifetime, and 1.2 percent in a given year. Among adolescents, 2.7 percent develop some kind of eating disorder. All of these disorders, by definition, are considered severe.[19]

Some specific eating disorders:

* anorexia nervosa

* binge-eating disorder

* bulimia nervosa

Family impact. Betty's two young children are scared for their mom. They hear from their grandparents and aunt that she is sick, but she doesn't really look sick to them. They don't understand what's wrong.

Betty's sister is angry. She knows that Betty has an eating disorder and is being "pigheaded" and "selfish" by not being a better role model for her children. She has confronted Betty several times about the way she eats and obsesses about her body, but Betty refuses to see it as a problem and makes promises to change but never does. Betty's sister has done much research on anorexia and is convinced that Betty needs to go to an inpatient residential facility as soon as possible. She wants her parents to pay for this, but her parents are not able to do so. Nobody knows what to do next. They are desperate because they believe Betty will die if she doesn't get help.

Mood disorders. William was a social worker for a city organization. Although the hours were long and the pay was low, he generally appreciated his job. But over the last couple of months, William has grown less content with life. He feels low and invisible. He feels as if his work is of little or no consequence, and he feels useless. His girlfriend grew increasingly frustrated with his whiny and pessimistic attitude, and when William said hurtful things to her and actually struck her in a rage during a fight, she left him. He felt like a complete loser.

William stopped taking care of his condo and started calling in sick a few times a month. Sometimes he sleeps until three o'clock in the afternoon because he just can't get out of bed. He was placed on probation at work due to poor performance.

One day he called in and quit his job over the phone. He's thought about killing himself because he feels life isn't worth living anymore.

Definition. Mood disorders primarily affect a person's emotional balance and well-being. People with mood disorders go through periods of depression and some also go through periods of mania, an extremely elevated emotional state. These periods of depression are more than the normal feelings of sadness or anger that we all go through. They are serious mood disturbances that interfere with function and may be debilitating.

Characteristics. Mood disorders are caused by imbalances in brain chemicals; they may be inherited genetically and may be triggered by circumstances—especially stress or grief. Mood disorders may make it impossible for a person to get out of bed or to sleep, to interact with others or to fulfill basic responsibilities. They may lose their appetite, have trouble concentrating or experience physical symptoms like headaches, stomachaches or joint pain. They may feel overwhelmed by negative feelings and may become suicidal.

People typically can't just "pull themselves out of" depression. At the same time, unfortunately, it's very difficult for many depressed people to get the help they need. Their mood may be so disrupted that they lack the energy or decision-making skills to seek help, or they may be so overwhelmed with feelings of worthlessness that they believe they don't deserve help.

Prevalence. According to the National Institute of Mental Health, in a twelve-month period 9.5 percent of adults in the United States experience a mood disorder. Of these, 45 percent are considered "severe."[20] Women are 50 percent more likely than men to develop a mood disorder.[21] These disorders are even more common in adolescents, with 14 percent experiencing a mood disorder annually.[22] The bulk of this is major depressive disorder, each year affecting 11 percent of people between the ages of thirteen and eighteen in the United States.

Some specific mood disorders:

- bipolar disorder

- depression

- dysthymic disorder

- major depressive disorder

Family impact. William's family has been frustrated with him for the past year. He's hard to be around because he seems self-centered, he always seems sad, and he complains that he has been given an unfair lot in life. The majority of the conversations William has with his parents and sister involve him crying and not listening to their advice. He won't go to a doctor. He won't tough it out. He won't get out there and date another woman. He just "stays in his house and mopes around all day." He sometimes says things that make them wonder if he might hurt himself.

Personality disorders. Sasha has had a colorful string of relationships over the past three years. She is currently twenty-seven and living with her new boyfriend—and madly in love. She has known her boyfriend for two months and believes he is "the one."

The boyfriend she was living with previously had become her fiancé a few months before. Unfortunately, that relationship was broken off when he expressed frustration over her controlling and confusing ways of getting what she wanted. She could be very attentive and kind one minute and then a vindictive, selfish "devil woman" the next. When her fiancé suggested that they do couples therapy, she flew off the handle and said that he was a wimpy, emasculated, no-good sissy boy and that she could never be married to a "little girl" like him. When he recovered from the verbal onslaught and said that he was no longer sure he wanted to be her husband, she said, "Great!" and left. She felt relieved to have discovered what he was really like before it was too late. The next week, Sasha met her current boyfriend, who's "absolutely perfect" for her. From a distance, Sasha's family has seen a pattern in her relationships, moving from one "perfect man" to the next every few months. As soon as the man she's dating complains about her efforts to control him, she decides he's a villain and moves on to the next man, whom she's sure is the right one.

This pattern reminds Sasha's family of her relationship with them, as she has constantly idealized or villainized them, begged them to be close or pushed them away bitterly. After a recent reconciliation, her family encouraged her to seek help from a therapist. But that only drove them apart again, and now she won't talk to any of them.

Definition. Personality disorders are mental illnesses that disrupt people's perceptions and behavior so pervasively, they constantly affect how they think and relate to others. In other words, these disorders are woven into people's personalities. Their symptoms are not episodic; instead, they are expressed in how people make decisions, engage in relationships and perceive the world daily and over a long period. These disorders are difficult to detect because the sufferers seem normal to themselves; therefore, they may have serious trouble functioning in society but blame others for their problems.

Characteristics. Personality disorders might sound like a convenient way to classify people we find strange or countercultural. And it is important to acknowledge the element of subjectivity involved in diagnosing personality disorders. Mental health professionals must take into account people's behavior within their own cultural contexts—not in reference to those professionals' cultural preferences or even necessarily the broader culture. This reality has caused some controversy over the definition and diagnosis of personality disorders.

Professionals diagnose personality disorders not just on the basis of behavior versus cultural norms, but also on the level of disruption to people's lives. People with personality disorders are not simply oddballs. They experience impaired functioning, particularly in relationships with other people and in coping with stressful circumstances. Personality disorders are thought to be caused by both genetic and environmental factors, and researchers have found strong links between personality disorders and the experience of abuse in childhood.[23]

Prevalence. According to the National Institute of Mental Health, in a twelve-month period 9 percent of US adults exhibit some kind of personality disorder.

Some specific personality disorders:

- antisocial personality disorder
- avoidant personality disorder
- borderline personality disorder
- histrionic personality disorder
- narcissistic personality disorder
- paranoid personality disorder
- schizotypal personality disorder

Family impact. Sasha's family tries to stay at arm's length from her. She is not a nice person to be around when she gets angry, and they have learned that not being around her works best for them. It seems like nothing will make her happy. She often explodes, apologizes, treats them nicely and then explodes again—too much drama for any of them. Her parents were glad when she moved out of the house to go to college, because she was so disruptive to their family. They feel guilty about this and are convinced that they did something wrong or that something terrible happened to her that she hasn't told them about.

Schizophrenia and other psychotic disorders. Bradley is a college student studying economics. He has always been personable and engaged in his studies. He has maintained a steady girlfriend for the past two years and is excited to graduate next year.

As this semester has progressed, he has grown increasingly frustrated with his friends, acquaintances and professors, believing they have intentionally tried to sabotage his ability to perform well in school. He also believes his girlfriend changed all the clocks in his apartment and his wristwatch to make him late for an exam. And he thinks his fraternity brothers turned against him and threw a party for a rival student who is pursuing the same internship he is, an internship that will lead to an excellent job after graduation. And one of his professors is visiting him late at night and giving him incorrect information to study.

The pressure of these assaults is gaining on Bradley, and he hasn't been sure what to do. He did file an ethical complaint about these conspiracies with the campus police. When the campus police were dismissive, Bradley became very frustrated and decided he had only one option. As he attempted to break into the university president's office suite, the campus police heard him saying over and over, "I have to shut it off."

Definition. Psychotic disorders are illnesses that cause serious disruption to people's perceptions of reality. When the symptoms are present, these disorders are disabling. They undermine people's ability to think normally, perceive what is true or present, and express emotion. These disorders are sensationalized in movies and television shows, and many people tend to think of their sufferers as "lost causes"; however, these disorders are treatable. Unfortunately, according to the World Health Organization, more than half of people with schizophrenia do not receive the care they need.[24]

Characteristics. People with psychotic disorders suffer from delusions (false beliefs) and hallucinations (false perceptions). Delusions may include paranoid beliefs that they are in danger. This paranoia may manifest itself in specific fears or a general sense of terror. Hallucinations may be auditory (such as hearing voices), visual (such as seeing people or things that aren't there) or involving other senses. People with psychotic disorders are not able to think or express their thoughts in an organized fashion, and they say and do things that others can't understand and that may be bizarre. Approximately 10 percent of people with schizophrenia commit suicide.

Prevalence. According to the National Institute of Mental Health, schizophrenia affects 1 percent of the US adult population.[25] Other psychotic disorders are uncommon, and prevalence is unclear for some; for all psychotic disorders the total prevalence is probably less than 1.5 percent of adults.[26]

Some specific psychotic disorders:

- brief psychotic disorder
- delusional disorder
- schizoaffective disorder
- schizophrenia

Family impact. Bradley's parents are in a state of shock because what they have heard does not make sense to them. Bradley has always been a responsible and respectful boy. He's never gotten into trouble and has always been mindful of others. They think someone must have slipped him some drugs, or maybe he's too stressed out over his studies. They're trying desperately to help Bradley feel safe, and they insisted that he move back in with them and take the semester off.

Unfortunately, the respite lasted only a short while after he came home from the hospital. After two months, Bradley is behaving strangely again. Even though he's going to therapy and is taking his meds, he has been acting increasingly paranoid and bizarre. He won't come out of his room under any circumstances. He will eat only ramen noodles, and he insists that his parents learn a password before they talk with him.

His father is at wits' end and has confronted Bradley severely a couple of times. His parents are terrified that he is not safe and wonder if they should call 911.

Time for a Change

In partnership with *Leadership Journal*, I conducted a survey of five hundred churches, using the National Alliance on Mental Illness (NAMI) definition of mental illnesses: "medical conditions that disrupt a person's thinking, feeling, mood, ability to relate to others and daily functioning" and "often result in a diminished capacity for coping with the ordinary demands of life." In this survey, 98.4 percent of respondents, who were pastors and other church leaders, indicated they are aware of mental illnesses or disorders among people in their congregations. (More on the results of this survey throughout the book.) If these church leaders are indicative of all—or even most—church leaders, nearly every church has recognized mental illness in its congregation.

The mentally ill might feel as if they are on the margins of society, but they're actually in the mainstream. And with the drugs available today—and improvements to come—mental illnesses can be treated and managed effectively for most people. And yet our *Leadership Journal* survey also found that only 12.5 percent of responding church leaders said mental illness is discussed openly and in a healthy way in their churches. Fifty percent said mental illness is mentioned in their church's sermons only one to three times per year; 20 percent said it is never mentioned.

Meanwhile, our culture at large is growing in its openness to acknowledging and discussing mental illness. It's becoming commonplace for celebrities to talk openly about their own struggles. Comedic actor Darrell Hammond has talked about self-injury stemming from abuse he experienced as a child.[28] Actress Kirsten Dunst shares openly about her experience with depression and claims that, although many people are embarrassed to talk about their struggles, it's "weird" for people not to go through depression.[29] Actress Catherine Zeta-Jones and journalist Jane Pauley have been open about their ongoing treatment for bipolar disorder.[30] Singer Brittany Spears captured the attention of paparazzi and mainstream media for days as she went through a public meltdown before receiving treatment for bipolar disorder.[31] NFL

IN 2010, I CONDUCTED A SURVEY among readers of *Leadership Journal* and other Christianity Today publications for church leaders. I asked them about their experiences with mental illness among members of their congregations, in their families and personally. I also asked them what their churches believe about mental illness, how they treat people with mental illness, how frequently they mention mental illness in their sermons and other revealing questions about this sensitive topic. Among five hundred responses, 98 percent have seen some type of mental illness in their congregation.[27]

- Eighty-four percent of church leaders are aware of some type of anxiety disorder within their congregation.

- Ninety-one percent of church leaders have seen mood disorders such as depression within their churches.

- Thirty-seven percent of church leaders indicated that someone in their congregation had suffered from a psychotic disorder such as schizophrenia.

- Of the church leaders in my survey, 38.7 percent indicated they had suffered from a mood disorder such as depression or bipolar disorder.

wide receiver Brandon Marshall announced that he had been diagnosed with borderline personality disorder and committed "to be the face of BPD. I'll make myself vulnerable if it saves someone's life."[32] A contestant on *American Idol*, seventeen-year-old Shelby Tweten, talked about living with bipolar disorder, saying, "I want to show people that bipolar disorder doesn't define who you are."[33] Actress Glenn Close has talked about the effect her sister's bipolar

- Twenty-three percent indicated they had suffered from an anxiety disorder, such as generalized anxiety disorder, post-traumatic stress disorder, obsessive-compulsive disorder, panic disorder or social anxiety disorder.

- Nine percent of church leaders indicated they had personally suffered from impulse control and addiction disorders such as pyromania, kleptomania, compulsive gambling, and alcohol and drug addictions.

- In my survey, 10.6 percent of church leaders indicated they had a family member who had suffered from a psychotic disorder such as schizophrenia. (According to the National Institute of Mental Health, 1.1 percent of the American population suffers from schizophrenia in a given year.)

- Church leaders who had suffered from mental illness indicated a much higher incidence of suffering within their families. For example, among those who had suffered from any kind of mental illness, 85 percent had family members suffering from mood disorders, compared with 56 percent of those who had not suffered from mental illness themselves.

disorder has had on her family, and she started a national campaign to end the stigma attached to mental illness.[34] And media of all kinds are beginning to deal more candidly and sensitively with issues of mental health and mental illness.

The church should not lag; it should lead the way. We serve a God who calls us to serve "the least of these" as if we were serving him (Mt 25:40). Jesus said, "Healthy people don't need a doctor—sick people do. I have come to call not those who think they are righteous, but those who know they are sinners" (Mk 2:17). As living temples carrying God's presence in this world, we must allow his light to shine out from us and infiltrate the darkness that surrounds so many people and drives some of them to despair.

Unfortunately, in many churches, we are afraid of the dark. We have lost our courage and conviction that light can conquer darkness. The darkness has cast itself over the light, and suffering people are not safe.

3

SUFFERING PEOPLE

My mom's earlier symptoms of schizophrenia are much more obvious in hindsight. When my siblings and I were young, she had trouble reading books or following sermons, focusing on what other people were saying to her and making decisions. She had difficulty starting or carrying on conversations, expressing her thoughts and relating to other people. And others sometimes had trouble understanding what she was trying to say. She also found herself unable to express emotions, both verbally and nonverbally. She exhibited some social withdrawal, avoiding gatherings or get-togethers with family or friends. She lacked close friendships, and Dad thought she sometimes lacked good judgment.

However, her illness was not fully developed, and it was not clear that she had a mental disorder. What changed that was a reaction to stress.

My father had left his position as pastor of a small church, and our family had moved from a rural community to a city. My brother, Scott, the oldest of four kids, had started college and was living away from home (although nearby), and my older sister, Cheryl, would soon follow. With three teenage girls at home, family dynamics were sometimes rocky. My parents' relationship became strained as well.

Dad had been out of work for months, filling temp jobs while he looked for another pastoral position. Mom, who had spent the last twenty years as a homemaker, had no work either. She was terrified by city traffic and overwhelmed by the challenge of negotiating a new community. Finances were strained to the point of poverty. We had found housing in the bottom floor of an old two-story house, with two bedrooms and one bathroom and some shady neighbors.

We were all making significant emotional and cultural adaptations—and struggling with the adjustments this transition required. For my mother, the stress of this time brought on the full-blown psychosis of schizophrenia, with symptoms that were impossible to ignore and that made her almost completely non-functioning. As I've mentioned, through the years that followed, she was hospitalized repeatedly, medicated heavily and inconsistent in taking her medication. So one crisis was layered on another, and my family struggled to cope.

For me, this crisis meant developing an extreme sense of independence and responsibility for myself and my younger sister, Kate. I felt an even stronger sense of responsibility to care for Mom in her suffering and to try to "make her better." It also meant tremendous confusion about what was happening to my mom and to my family, a sense of shame that kept me silent and recurring grief that was so overwhelming at times, I had to lay my heart and soul aside when I went out into the world beyond our front door. My siblings had responses both similar to mine and unique to them.

The day my brother found Mom in a psychosomatic paralysis—her means of coping with her internal conflict between reality and delusion—was as traumatic for him as it was confusing and frightening for me. Of this time, Scott says, "I didn't have a clue how to respond. I was filled with a fear of what I didn't understand. I think the trauma was much worse for me than if it would have been a physical injury that I could at least understand."

Like mine, my brother's sense of responsibility inflated—and exploded into guilt. Although he was the first to experience the trauma of finding Mom in an incoherent state, because he was away from home he escaped much of the direct experience of living with a mentally ill parent. He says, "Since the most severe problems began after I was away from home, I have felt unmerited guilt that I was the only one who escaped without having to live as a teenager in a home with a mother who was severely mentally ill. I often feel pain as I think of the pain that my sisters lived through, and it makes it worse that I was somewhat removed from it."

Interestingly, this strong sense of responsibility and guilt arose in my older sister, Cheryl, as well. Without knowing that Scott was feeling responsible for all of us and I was feeling responsible for myself and my younger sister, she felt responsible for everyone and strove to take the burden on herself as much as she could to protect the people she loved.

Our home life revolved around protecting ourselves and preserving Mom's peace. Cheryl knew we needed to protect Mom's feelings and keep her from getting upset:

> If there was a conflict, what mattered was not the truth of the event or our true feelings, but resolving it quickly in a manner that appeased Mom's feelings. It has always been, and continues to be, very difficult for me to be honest about my thoughts or feelings, especially if they may be in conflict with anyone else's. I definitely shut down emotionally because acknowledging my feelings would require me to admit to them, and that would be too difficult.

Kate, the youngest, also tried to "fix" Mom. Twelve years old at the time, she remembers "trying to figure out what was actually wrong with her, like a puzzle, because I wasn't satisfied with the explanations we were given, but at the same time I didn't really want to know." Kate says that each time Mom went to the hospital,

I purged the house of anything she had touched that I might
come in contact with. Some of it was real cleaning, like
washing all the towels, doing the dishes, scrubbing the
counters and toilets. Others were not so direct, like throwing
out all the prepared and opened food that I thought she
would have touched—just erasing her existence in any way I
could and pretending she was never coming back.

Dad, already feeling low and inadequate as he struggled through
long-term unemployment and then underemployment, sank into
depression. He wondered how to help his family and himself. He
needed help, but as he says, "With mental illness, you don't have a
cast on your head or anything else to show that you're a hurting
person who needs sympathy."

Because we were all in crisis individually, protecting and preserving ourselves as best we could, we didn't openly reach out to
one another and develop solidarity. Scott felt guilty: "I was the only
one who escaped." Cheryl "shut down emotionally." And Kate was
busy "purging the house" and "pretending [Mom] was never
coming back." Instead of pulling together, we tried to make life as
normal as possible, while worrying constantly about what would
come next and about how each other member of the family was
coping. The difficulty of growing up this way put distance between
us just when we most needed each other. We desperately needed
an outside voice to lovingly name our trouble and call us together.

Ways We Suffer

Families directly affected by mental illness are in crisis. This is
always true, regardless of whether the family consists of two people
or fifty; whether the family is close or scattered; and whether
mental illness strikes a child, a parent or a grandparent. The exact
nature, length and degree of crisis vary widely, but families report
several common elements. Because members of these families are

showing up at churches every weekend, it's critical that people in the church understand what's going on in their lives and hearts. What follows is a description of some of the ways people suffer, along with stories in their own words.

Special rules. Mental illness changes the rules for maintaining family peace. Other family members find themselves bending around the person with mental illness, adapting and suppressing their own personalities and independence in an effort to keep the ill person stable and happy.

In my family, this meant sometimes taking upon ourselves things that Mom used to do—like cooking Sunday dinner. At other times, it meant letting Mom do it even though it took her 200 percent longer and she didn't always get it right. It meant hiding our feelings, not inviting friends over or introducing them to our parents, subtly keeping an eye on the bottles to see whether Mom was taking her meds and keeping the peace by following bizarre rules Mom would establish but couldn't explain.

Just as ours did, many homes revolve around the needs of one person. Like Cheryl, who "knew that we needed to protect Mom's feelings," another woman I spoke with said her home was full of rules for preserving her mother's equilibrium, like "don't let Mom read the *Enquirer*, because it might give her funny ideas."

Resource monopoly. As with other illnesses, the sick person demands much of the family's resources, with little left for those who are well. The family is drained emotionally, physically and often financially. Deprived of what they need, individuals learn to adapt or resent the loved one—or both.

I spoke with a psychologist who put it this way: "With the time and energy that it takes, the ill person often becomes the focus and center, so how does the family keep balance? Some family members can get overlooked and their concerns put to the side."

My friend Monica said this about her teenage daughter's

struggle to learn to manage depression and borderline person-ality disorder: "Everything in our lives revolved around her: how do we keep her safe, how do I help her, what exactly is going on, why is it getting worse and not better? It overtook our lives, over-shadowed pretty much everything. Everything else was on auto-pilot in comparison to that."

The person with mental illness becomes an emotional black hole, with the feelings and needs of everyone else swirling around him or her. Medical intervention, especially hospitalization and residential treatment, can consume the entire family budget and more. Navigating the requirements of insurance companies and advocating for loved ones can be a full-time job. When a family member is hospitalized, visits take a lot of time—not to mention the serious emotional toll. When Mom was incarcerated in the state hospital when transitioning from her prison term, Dad drove sixty miles each way at least once a week to visit her. Not everyone can manage this—and for those who can, it's exhausting.

This kind of resource reallocation takes place in other families where chronic illness or dysfunction are present, and it should be expected in the presence of serious illness. But because mental illness goes so frequently undiagnosed or un-acknowledged, the support system often isn't strong enough to counterbalance the demands. And rather than making a short-term adaptation, families often find themselves perma-nently maladjusted.

Confusion. When a mental illness first shows its symptoms, no one, including the person struggling with the illness, understands what's happening. Depending on the illness, the sick family member may be confused by paranoia and delusions—which in turn can confuse everyone else. When my mom started showing symptoms, Dad was confused by her actions, which sometimes didn't make sense, and by her attempts to communicate with him, which were occasionally impossible to understand.

A friend of mine, who suffered with a severe anxiety disorder for three years before getting it under control, was in the middle of a job interview when she had her first panic attack. She says, "The walls felt like they were closing in on me, my heart raced, I couldn't think straight or pay attention to what the interviewer was saying. I wanted desperately to run from the room. I felt hysterical inside, like I was losing total control. I had no idea what was happening."

She didn't get that job, but did find another job elsewhere, and the panic attacks continued and grew in frequency until she experienced them regularly throughout the workday. This went on for weeks before she finally told her husband what was going on, and he encouraged her to see a doctor.

If a family receives professional help, they may find themselves even more confused by murky diagnoses, no diagnosis or multiple diagnoses at the hands of various professionals who make their assessments on the symptoms they see at the time, often without the benefit of an understanding of the person's history. These families often don't receive much guidance on how to help the suffering person, and what they tried yesterday may not work today (more on this in the "Navigating the System" section in the next chapter). And the church and culture may send them confusing messages about what causes mental illness and how they should respond.

Children especially fall victim to general confusion and may develop their own inaccurate explanations to try to make sense of their reality. One woman I spoke with said, "My dad used to say, 'Your mother is weak, she just can't handle things.' So I thought, *I'd better be strong. I don't want to cry, because maybe somebody will take me away.* I had it in my mind that this only happened to women. You know, women who cry might be taken away."

Anxiety. Because the symptoms of many mental illnesses tend to repeat in cycles, families spend a lot of time and energy anticipating the next cycle, waiting for the next round, watching for signs that a loved one is losing grip on reality, retreating into a dark place or engaging in self-harm. They try to make sure the sufferer is taking her or his prescribed medications. They work to anticipate, contain and minimize disruptive behavior. Sometimes they just try to get the person out of bed for a while or to keep him or her from starving to death or committing suicide. And, while in constant emotional turmoil, they try to go on with life, interacting with people in "the rest of the world" whom they believe don't understand.

One woman described her family's coping when she was growing up:

> Because of the silence, my brothers and sisters, we learned to pick on each other. We were in so much individual pain that we didn't learn how to come together as a family. We suffered silently. I bit my nails a lot; I showed signs of anxiety. Three out of six kids were bed wetters later in life. Again, a sign of stress. I was extremely overweight as a teenager because . . . I found food to be the coping mechanism.

My sister Cheryl is now an adult, with her own family and responsibilities, yet she says,

> [I've had] constant anxiety over what Mom will do next, when she will stop taking her medication and why, who she might harm, how she will embarrass us, how I will get her help and where, where she can live. We have always had to be concerned about how she will be provided for financially, how to have insurance cooperate with the care she needs, what kind of job she can have to feel useful and not sit around all the time, and what living arrangement she can have with enough structure and monitoring for her meds and lifestyle.

My friend Monica describes keeping vigil for days, trying to keep her daughter from self-harm or suicide: "You put away the sharp things, but you can't put away everything. I hid the knives and the scissors and things I thought she could hurt herself with, and she would just find something else." Before her daughter's first hospitalization, Monica tried a constant watch at home. Her daughter had to have someone with her twenty-four hours a day—a huge challenge for Monica, a single parent. "I didn't shower for a few days, and she had a bed set up in my room. She was tired of me and angry with me, and it was a very unpleasant, difficult time. It was just a crisis, and it was a matter of keeping her alive. She said, 'If you would just leave me alone, I would kill myself, so just leave me alone.'"

Another parent, a father whose son was diagnosed with bipolar disorder as a teenager, said, "When we do lie down, we're not sleeping well. It's not my work that keeps me up. It's my son that I think about. That impacts the way you function; it impacts the way you relate to your loved ones. You need people to come alongside you to say, 'Yeah, that happens to me but we found this to work.'"

My friend Marlena, whose father suffers from bipolar disorder, described her anxiety when he was out of control in a manic episode that lasted nearly six months: "During that time, we lived in a war zone. At any moment, I felt like Dad could step on a landmine and blow us all to smithereens. I never knew what to expect. I lived and slept on edge. Every time the phone rang, I tensed up, fearing the worst. I could barely function for fear of what he might accidentally do to himself, our family or others."

She also loses sleep over the fear that her young daughter might inherit the same disorder. "In those dark hours, I wonder if my sweet, precocious little girl will suffer as my father has when her hormones kick in. It's my biggest fear."

Guilt. Especially for parents whose children struggle with mental illness, guilt becomes a nagging companion. One psychologist I spoke with described this as "parental guilt that they weren't proactive. 'How could I not have picked up on that?' 'We should have done more.' They feel inadequacy or failure on their part. Then shame and guilt come out of it."

Trudy Weiss is the mother of David Weiss, a young man who has been diagnosed with schizophrenia and who has been courageous enough to write about his experiences in *Christianity Today* and on his own blog. Trudy also has written some of her reflections on David's illness, published on his blog. She speaks of this parental guilt:

> I repented of being a closet democrat, I would become a republican. I decided to like everyone and hate none. I knew I had caused this because I occasionally yelled when I got angry. I repented of everything I could think of and then started playing "Let's Make a Deal." God, heal my son and take my life instead. Or heal my son and I will read the Bible every day. Even, heal my son and I will never gossip again.[1]

Because of the responsibility parents naturally feel for their kids and because our culture automatically points the finger at parents of kids with problems, they wonder: Was it something I did? Failed to do? Is God punishing my family? Did I cause this, and if so, why can't I fix it?

Maladjustment. For children who themselves suffer with mental illness, childhood is not what it should be. They struggle to fit in and to understand themselves; they often interpret the world around them through a skewed lens. Without early recognition and intervention, a mentally ill child may have a lifelong struggle ahead.

My brother-in-law Kevin, who has waged a lifelong battle with depression, as a child remained silent about his hardships because he was ashamed and desperately feared disappointing his family. He describes his feelings leading up to a suicide attempt in elementary school: "I decided to try to end my life. In my heart I wanted people to see I was hurting. I know what I did was very selfish. There was also an ignorant part of me that just wanted it to end." He thought suicide would not affect his family, "because they would know I was with God, and besides, I would be less of a pain if I was not around."

For children of parents with mental illness, especially serious illness, life is built on a shifting foundation, which may leave them confused about who they are, emotionally starved, alienated from the "normal" world around them, ashamed and at risk of their own problems with mental illness, substance abuse and other complications.

In the book *Growing Up with a Schizophrenic Mother*, Margaret J. Brown and Doris Parker Roberts cite a survey in which more than 25 percent of people with schizophrenic mothers reported that they had problems with alcohol, drugs or both at some point. They exhibited school dysfunction, rebelliousness, trouble with eating and illnesses, promiscuous behavior, violence and other ways of acting out.[2] And research indicates that anyone with a mentally ill parent has an increased risk of developing mental illness. This increased risk is due in part to genetic factors and in part to the environment and parent-child relationship that develop under the influence of the parent's illness. Children of people with schizophrenia have a 13 percent chance of developing schizophrenia themselves, while the risk for the general population is less than 1 percent.[3]

If a parent is hospitalized, especially repeatedly, the children may not understand why that parent is gone and may miss her or him tremendously. Even if parents are not functioning well enough to provide their children with good care, children still desperately love and need their parents.

I spoke with one woman who told a heartbreaking story from her childhood of welcoming her mother back from her first hospitalization. She didn't understand what had happened but had missed her mom so much:

And here I am with this gigantic smile because my mom is home, and I remember being kind of surprised because when she came in the door she didn't have a smile on her face. She didn't look sad; she just had a blank look on her face, not emotional. She walked upstairs into the living room, sat in her favorite rocking chair, and just stared and stared out the picture window. I followed her up the stairs and just stood right next to her in her rocking chair. Just her physical presence being home was comforting. Even if she wasn't reaching out to me, hugging me, whatever, just her physical presence.

This young girl desperately needed her mother and was confused but comforted by her presence. Long-term adaptation to such encounters changes children's expectations for what they can and should receive from their parents and others. It can also drive them to try to find elsewhere what they should be getting at home—trying to satisfy emotional needs they may not even know they have. My friend Angie talks about her "tendency to latch on to somebody": "I felt like I had this nurture deficit growing up because I was the one having to really be the parent, the mature person in the family emotionally."

Role reversal. If the person with mental illness is a caregiver, the onset of symptoms usually means a role reversal within the family, as the ill person now requires significant care from the family, at least for a time. If the suffering person is a parent, children may be forced to grow up quickly and "parent" the parent.

Angie, whose adoptive parents struggled with borderline personality disorder and attachment disorder, remembers "just taking it on myself and feeling so responsible." She added, "I didn't enjoy childhood as much as I think I could have or should have." Another woman said, "I thought, 'I can fix her. I can make her happy.' So as a little girl, I'm setting the table in the morning, I'm cleaning the house because I'm thinking I can make her feel better."

The sense of responsibility this engenders may last for that child's lifetime—for good and for bad. And it may mean an end to childhood.

Instability. For a family touched by mental illness, life is unpredictable and may be all about survival. Everyone—the ill person and anyone caring for or depending on that person—has to redefine what life looks like. In my dad's words, as he described how he felt in realizing my mother was suffering from a serious mental illness, "Our future plans were down the drain."

The greatest level of instability is for the person with mental illness. David Weiss describes this from the perspective of someone with schizophrenia:

> There are things I have learned over the years of battling mental illness. The first is my emotions are liars. There are times when my sadness, anxiety, fear, and even anger are out of control. Sometimes reality itself seems to have turned on its head. Suddenly I can hear God telling [me] to evangelize to everyone in a certain hotel, or that my super suction shoes let me walk up walls, or God wants [me] to take a "leap of faith" off the roof of my house. Or the disease can manifest itself a different way. I may see something on TV that makes me so mad that I want to lug the TV outside and run it over with my car or even assume that a loved one hates me because they looked at me a certain way.[4]

This instability extends to everyone else in the family. One woman recalled the instability of family life:

> When I was ten years old, my mom came into my bedroom in the middle of the night and whispered into my ear that my dad was trying to poison me. I remember being really startled. I went upstairs to the bathroom, shut and locked the door, and said to myself, "Is my dad really trying to hurt me, or is something the matter with my mom?" I remembered that my mom had been crying a lot a few days before; she was pacing

back and forth between the kitchen and the living room. She had this really distressed look on her face; she thought she was getting secret messages from the radio and the TV. The next day my mom was gone, and nobody sat us six kids down to tell us what had happened.

Angie describes her childhood this way:

My personality is the responsible oldest one, so I was the fixer in the family, trying to get Mom and Dad to talk, and I just hated when there was conflict. My brother and sister would withdraw and deal with it in their own ways. My mom was very volatile; my dad was disengaged. They would go for days with the silent treatment, which just drove me crazy, trying to make something happen so they would talk to each other. Then she would get into these bouts of being sad that nobody was meeting her needs or something. I have memories of incidents like when she locked herself in the bathroom with a knife and was threatening to kill herself, and my dad was just fed up with it and sitting outside in his easy chair. And I'm like, "Aren't you going to do something? Does nobody else see something going on here?"

Marlena had a chaotic childhood. During her father's untreated manic episodes, he went on spending sprees and engaged in immoral behavior. He went AWOL from the military when she was a child and later served time in a military prison. He had an affair with an eighteen-year-old college student and impulsively bought a two-seated red sports car (he had a family of six).

On a given day, simply getting out of bed may be the only accomplishment for someone with active symptoms. For others, affirming reality may be the only victory. Or keeping a loved one alive. Or quelling a panic attack. People who are just trying to stay afloat are not well equipped to handle crashing waves. Their boats rock, take on water and sometimes capsize. And they may never be able to right them without help.

Meds. Ah, the push-pull of medication. The blessing and the curse. It sounds simple: go to the doctor, get the right medication, keep taking it, and you'll be fine. If only it were as simple and effective as it sounds. It's true that meds are extremely helpful and even critical for many people who suffer from mental illness. It's also true that significant advances in medicine have improved these medications dramatically in recent years. But finding the right medication remains a mysterious process for most people and their doctors; typically a great deal of experimentation precedes the serendipitous discovery of the right "cocktail."

Bob Mills, associate vice president of advancement at Wake Forest University, has been diagnosed with bipolar disorder and describes his as a mild case. He takes only two medications (in contrast with many people who have a mental illness, who must take several). And even for him, the process of finding the right antidepressant took a year. For people who have a more serious illness or multiple diagnoses, it can take much longer.

Once a person is stabilized on the right meds, he or she may still struggle with some degree of symptoms. These medications are not perfect solutions. It's also important to understand that these medications can be incredibly expensive and can produce side effects that hobble a person's functioning and make him or her miserable.

Some people with mental illness refuse to maintain consistency in taking their meds. We call these people "noncompliant," and they produce intense frustration and repeated heartbreak in the people who love them. My family has experienced this heartbreak as Mom has not been faithful in taking her meds. That choice is understandable; her health and her quality of life truly have suffered from the side effects of drugs. And because powerful antidepressants and antipsychotic drugs suppress so much of a person's thinking and feeling, she has felt like a shell of herself. Even though the medicine made her seem more normal to the rest of the world, she has sometimes felt that her psychotic state was normal and her medicated state seemed strange. Normal thoughts seemed false and boring. So she would stop taking medication, and every time she would spin downward again and end up hospitalized.

I spoke with a director at the National Alliance on Mental Illness (NAMI), a support and advocacy organization for people affected by mental illness. She works hard to educate community leaders and public officials—including police officers—about mental illness. She told me, "The number-one question the police ask us is why people don't stay on their medication." She asks them to consider, as an example, one antipsychotic medication that causes twenty to one hundred pounds of weight gain. "Would you, in our body-conscious culture, willingly take a medicine that causes you to gain twenty to one hundred pounds?" With the weight gain might come a secondary diagnosis: diabetes. Now the person is taking the antipsychotic plus insulin. When symptoms worsen, she or he goes to the hospital and receives a shot of Haldol to clear up the psychosis. As a side effect, the Haldol produces very stiff muscles, so the patient has to take Cogentin so the muscles can loosen. It goes on and on—so many side effects and expensive medications.

Sometimes people simply do not recognize their illness and therefore their need for medication. But other times, they cannot afford their medications or feel they cannot endure the complications that come with taking them. This does not excuse people who need medication from taking it. It might, however, engender some empathy for them and point to one way churches can help (more on that in chapter eight).

Grief and loss. Mental illness is a robber. It robs suffering people of at least a small piece of who they are—even during a short-term illness. And it robs the people who love them—and the world—of healthy, clear-eyed and beautiful personalities made in the image of God. It robs families of life-giving relationships with people who always love them back. And it replaces those relationships with deep sadness over the new reality.

I feel this kind of loss every day. Some days it's more acute: Mother's Day is tough, especially sitting through sermons that idealize mothers' roles in our lives. Baby showers and births are hard; all my friends had their moms by their sides, and mine was nowhere near. Being a mom is difficult; I have a lot of self-doubt over whether I'm doing what "normal" moms do.

I've had many conversations with people who have spoken of this loss and the sadness they feel, starting with my own family. My sister Kate talks about her ongoing grief decades after we first lost mom to schizophrenia: "As an adult," she says, "I have grieved the loss of a mother and the loss of hope for the relationship that I always craved to have with my mother."

My sister Cheryl expresses it this way:

> The most painful times of my life involved visiting Mom in homeless shelters, sitting in courtrooms as she was tried and sentenced, and visiting her in jail. It was so conflicting to know she put herself there by her actions, but to imagine the despair she must feel to know she had fallen so far by fault of a mental illness which impaired her ability to reason logically without her medication.

My friend Angie talks about the impact of this loss on her parenting: "I feel like I'm working without a family legacy or model. So my husband and I have kind of started over in our own thing, and hopefully my kids will get the benefit of that. I feel lonely, I guess, sometimes. Even though I have very good relationships, there's still this feeling that I'm not connected to something bigger."

David Weiss's sister, Anna, grieved the loss of her brother when his schizophrenia affected his ability to function as the big brother she had known. She eloquently described this loss in an essay as a teenager, which David has reprinted on his blog:

> My mom and dad are still debating whether to send my brother away. Our life at home is an emotional rollercoaster with David's behavior changing every day and sometimes varying during the day. During the first year of his illness, I often looked at [a] picture of David and remembered the wonderful and sheltered years of childhood that we shared together. However, when I moved away from home for a while, I lost the picture. I wish that I could find it because it is the perfect example of my brother caring for me and protecting me. Now I am the one protecting and sheltering. I have become the older child with more responsibility, a job I was always thankful not to have.[5]

One man said this of the experience of sitting in church with his son, who has bipolar disorder: "The church has divorce groups, grief groups. Well, in some ways what we're dealing with here is divorce, is grief, and yet the kid's sitting right next to me."

This is a serious loss—the kind that redefines life as we know it and throws a deep shadow over life as we thought we might know it someday. Individuals and families need to grieve that loss— sometimes repeatedly, sometimes daily. For families affected by a long-term, serious, maybe lifelong illness, this grief is always fresh, never behind them. Every time an ill loved one suffers a relapse, drains the life out of someone, creates a public spectacle, can't get out of bed, zones out on medication, disappears, goes to jail or is represented by the empty chair at the family celebration, family members suffer too. And they grieve.

This ongoing pain keeps the wounds in people's hearts open—a condition God can use, but one that is excruciating. If you are waiting for someone to "get over" this kind of repeated loss, please give it up. Realize and accept that no one ever gets over this. The only remedy is redemption through God's grace, which provides a healing much different from getting over it (for more on that, see chapter nine).

Shame. On top of all this, when these families turn on the TV, watch a movie or engage in everyday conversation with "normal" people, they're reminded that in our society, which treats the mentally ill as jokes, terrifying criminals or subhuman, they are not considered normal and they are not wanted. This stigma and the resulting shame go beyond the person with mental illness and extend to the family. They believe that they're alone and that they ought to keep their family life a secret (more on the stigma of mental illness in chapter seven).

My family experienced this. In chapter one, I described my public humiliation in a dentist's office. My dad talks about his shame over "my wife saying or doing things that were not appropriate." He also talks about his desire for others to accept his wife even though she's ill. "Instead of that they shunned her and at times avoided talking to me. People with other illnesses, like cancer, were not shunned like my wife was."

Kate said about Mom, "I always wanted to be opposite of her. It has always been hard not feeling like I was normal. In retrospect I think this may be a normal feeling to most people, but I think it was pronounced in my life because I didn't have a natural, healthy relationship with my mother. One of my most important goals in life became to find normal."

Another woman talked about the effect of her mother's bipolar disorder: "Our family had a secret. We weren't to tell anybody. We weren't to talk about it with the neighbors, we weren't to talk about it at school, and we certainly didn't talk about it at church."

She recalls an incident of public humiliation when she was sixteen years old:

I was at home, the phone rang, and it was the manager from Kmart. My mom had been shopping erratically, the police were there, and it was clear that somebody needed to come and pick her up. I remember getting this really sick feeling in my stomach—here we go again. And I thought to myself, *When I go into the store I'm going to close my eyes, I'm going to keep my head down because I don't want to look at anybody rolling their eyes at her or laughing. . . .*

When I got to the back office at Kmart, there my mom was in a chair, just sobbing. And there was the cart, and it was just filled with stuff that made no sense, overflowing. It was as if she had run up and down the aisles and put it in. And I remember this really tall police officer just standing there.

All I ever wanted somebody to say to me was that they were going to take really good care of my mom. I felt a sense of humiliation, needing to go and pick her up. I can't say what it felt to be her, except her crying; I believe she felt that humiliation too. And when we walked out, I knew my mom was going to need to go to the hospital again.

My friend Marlena talks about the downward spiral of her bipolar father during an extended manic episode: "He was drinking and driving, getting into fistfights at bars, claiming he was a spy, asking everyone for money and allegedly sleeping with a girl half his age. He quit the job he held for many years, leaving himself and my mom homeless and destitute. He was out of control; no one wanted him around. He was the town's local freak show."

My brother-in-law Kevin describes the shame and alienation he felt during and after his first hospitalization during his senior year at a Christian college:

I had my psychotic breakdown on a Saturday while some friends were with me playing video games in our room. I don't remember much from that day. I can remember being taken to the hospital and thinking people were out to get us. We got to the hospital and my friends explained how I wanted to kill myself and I was paranoid. I awoke in a room with just a mattress. It was here that I gathered my thoughts and wondered what everyone thought of me. I thought, *My parents don't know. What are they going to think?* I wanted to die so bad after these thoughts that I banged on the door of the room and no one answered. So I decided to bang my head against the wall, and two nurses came running in and took me to another room and strapped me down to a bed. *What are people going to think now?*

After a long time passed, the door swung open, and my father was there. I wanted to hide in the corner so bad and run away from him. There was no hiding this anymore; I had come out of the mental closet for the world to see. I was embarrassed for him and for me.

Things were different at school after that. My friends alienated me, and I lost many friends. I was crushed; I never hurt them in any way. My roommate wanted out; he didn't want to be with me in the same room. So I moved around often.

It's hard to imagine our society attaching this kind of shame to any other genetically and environmentally based illnesses. Even AIDS and other sexually transmitted diseases do not bring condemnation, as we have focused more on compassion and treatment—and we acknowledge that many who suffer from these diseases are children and other secondhand victims. But we continue to judge people with mental illness for developing illnesses and disorders of the mind.

No one chooses mental illness, yet we persist in shunning sufferers, laughing at them and accepting their sense of shame as if it were warranted. And in case you believe this sense of shame is present only in the "worldly" culture around us, think again. It is alive and well within the church—with its own spiritual twists (for more on this, see chapter five).

Spiritual crisis. For people with mental illness and their families, the onset of symptoms and the ongoing suffering challenges faith—no matter how deeply rooted. And sometimes this crisis breaks a person's faith altogether, particularly if that person turns to the church for help and doesn't receive it or receives deeply hurtful treatment.

For many ill people, like those who suffer from other ailments, one of the first reactions may be to question God. Bob talks about coming down from a manic high and sinking into depression, feeling "pretty angry at God and saying, 'God, what in the world are you doing? I mean, here I was on this high and thinking that I'm called and all this stuff, and now I'm in the pit. This isn't any way to run Christianity. What are you up to?'"

For a delusional person, spiritual crisis may be part of the illness itself. Such a person may or may not seek spiritual help for this crisis and may not be capable of discerning truth from lies. Satan certainly will use any opportunity to lead a person away from faith in Christ— as he did with my mom. When she began to go astray and embrace the occult, it was after decades of knowing Christ and engagement in the church. This started with thinking that is typical for people with schizophrenia and other psychotic disorders. Regarding her experiences of delusion during church services, she says,

> I thought I had some special insights. There were hidden meanings in what I was hearing in church. It seemed that the truth which I had believed for so long was no longer accurate. Because of the secret information I was receiving in my thinking, I began to think, *I just don't believe this way anymore.* The "mysterious" became so appealing to me.
>
> My medication was not working properly for at least two to three years. I didn't realize that, and my family didn't either. I never said anything to anyone about the secret messages I

was supposedly getting. These were delusions. But I thought they were spiritual gifts and the Lord had drawn me close. I remained that way in our evangelical church for two full years before leaving the church.

After diving deeply into the occult, Mom has since rejected such beliefs and returned to faith in Christ. But for the rest of the family, Mom's spiritual crisis became our own as we wrestled with spiritual questions we had never discussed in Sunday school.

My brother, Scott, who holds a master's of divinity, explains: "It never caused me to doubt what I held true, but it rocked the very foundations of my world to find that Mom was no longer who I thought she was. I struggled deeply with a nagging question: Was she in the occult because of a conscious decision to abandon her faith, or was she simply deceived by the sick condition of her mind?" For him, this question had profound theological implications—he was concerned about the final destiny of her soul.

Scott describes his wrestling with these spiritual questions:

> In a way I want her bad decisions to be coming from her mental illness because I can explain them away more easily. At other times it seems easier if it's just coming from her sinful nature because then I can simply blame her and have somewhere to direct my anger. At the very least it would be nice if it was clearly one or the other. What I don't like is the possibility that the two could be so completely mixed together that it's impossible to tell which is primary at any one time.

David Weiss's mother, Trudy, describes her spiritual reaction to the onset of David's schizophrenia:

> I had a thousand questions and only a silent God to answer them. He owed me. I reminded him we were a good family; I had taken care of my dying mother-in-law. David and Anna visited her every day on their way home from school. We had

taken mission trips with our kids; we did without the big vacations so we had money to give away for worthy causes. I worked in a Christian school and believed in Christian Education. My family lived in America and God knows He loves Americans best.[6]

For those whose faith doesn't break, wrestling through tenacious and troubling questions may actually build faith, even if the wrestling never produces clear and satisfactory answers. But people need support.

It's important to understand that when a person is hospitalized or receives treatment from a counselor, that treatment may or may not reinforce the suffering person's Christian faith. It may actually lead them astray. For example, when Mom has been in the hospital and in day-treatment programs, some of her group leaders have used Christian principles in their group activities. But many have ignored the spiritual, and some have been hostile to faith. One even advocated occult activities in her group meetings. This was very confusing for Mom, who, like all people in her position, was extremely vulnerable.

Wrestling with these questions in the context of a supportive church—where faith is deep and honest enough to acknowledge that life in a sinful world is painful and twisted and that some questions don't have answers this side of heaven—could make a huge difference in determining whether the questions destroy or develop faith.

But for now, let's keep our attention outside the church and take a close look at the kind of help families receive from the mental health care system and their own efforts to cope.

4

COPING

In a mental health crisis, families often look for help in two places simultaneously: the mental health care system and their own coping mechanisms, designed to help them survive trouble that might otherwise overwhelm them. Unfortunately, both of these support systems frequently fail to provide what families need.

Navigating the System

When a mental illness has disrupted life for ill people—and their families—to the point where they seek treatment, they may find a whole new kind of suffering. Sadly, the system created to provide treatment and meet the needs of those in a mental health crisis sometimes creates new problems. It was not designed to do what most people need it to do. William Anthony, executive director of the Center for Psychiatric Rehabilitation at Boston University, says, "For the last 100 years, it was designed to help people who were going to deteriorate. Now we need a mental health system that facilitates folks who are going to recover."[1]

Because many church leaders believe their role in a mental health crisis is simply to refer people to appropriate professional care, it's important for them to understand that the system they are sending people into can be nearly impossible to navigate, and those walking through it need pastoral care. The system will not provide what the church can and must provide.

Psychology is not an exact science. Brain science is still in its infancy. No one completely understands the connections between the body, the mind and the spirit. Mental health professionals, especially counselors who are not administering medications, are free to develop their own theories and use their judgment in designing treatment plans for their clients. Most of these professionals are quite skilled and facilitate healing in the lives of the people they treat. Others, not so much. And there's no quack-o-meter out there to tell us whether we're walking into the office of someone without the knowledge or skills necessary to help.

Believe me, I have much respect for the highly qualified and gifted among them—my husband is one of them. And I have benefitted tremendously from the ministries of Christian counselors God has placed in my life. But even extremely skilled professionals can get in over their heads or fail to understand someone who has come to them for help. And because privacy laws require that mental health professionals' treatment plans rely almost exclusively on information presented by the person seeking help, they may be mistaken or even deceived if a patient is delusional, paranoid or manipulative.

For my own family, the mental health treatment system has been both blessing and bane. I've mentioned my mom's repeated hospitalizations, which have been traumatizing for everyone involved (more on that soon). I've mentioned Mom's time in prison, which most people probably don't realize is part of the system for mental health care in this country (more coming on this as well).

Mom has seen several counselors and psychiatrists, each with a unique approach. Some of them have been quite helpful, especially when she has faithfully taken her medication. Others have wasted her time and money with useless—or even counterproductive—

methods. For example, one counselor suggested that she journal about her thoughts, feelings and memories as a form of therapy. This became an obsessive exercise for her—she journaled constantly—and caused her to withdraw further into herself and her delusions. She fixated on her internal experiences and even invented many "memories" that, in Scott's words, "really just distracted us [her family and counselors] from the real issues for several months or even years."

Another source of frustration was the process of finding the right practitioners. The phone book provides a long list of qualified therapists, but it reveals almost nothing about their areas of expertise, their viewpoints on faith and their personalities. Contacting the insurance company will tell you who is in its network, but that list may not include anyone you feel you can trust. Without a strong network, someone who needs a counselor or psychiatrist can be easily and quickly overwhelmed by the attempt to find the right one. And if more than one professional is involved, they may not coordinate well with one another. Each time Mom started with a new therapist, she had to repeat her life story. She grew frustrated in feeling as if she couldn't get beyond the facts with anyone.

We aren't the only ones bewildered by this system, and the difficulties go far beyond the challenge of finding the right counselor or finding money to pay the psychiatrist. Aside from long-term therapy, the system focuses exclusively on stabilization and medication of patients and keeping people safe for the short term. It is reluctant to "label" people with diagnoses and bound by privacy laws from sharing any information, without written consent, with family members, who are then left to guess at how to support their loved one's treatment and ongoing health. If the ill person is expected to manage his or her own care and is noncompliant with medications, the family learns to expect chaos with each new day.

No one is allowed to force care on another person, except under the most extreme circumstances. Until a person is deemed a clear danger to self or others, nothing can be done to ensure that an unwilling family member receives care. This regulation is in place for good reason—to respect the rights of the individual and to prevent abuse—but it does create trouble for families struggling to help someone who clearly needs help but can't see or acknowledge that need.

Once people do get to the point of endangering themselves or others, a call to the police or a trip to the hospital thrusts them suddenly much further into a system they may not have yet learned to navigate. This was the case for my friend Monica, whose teenage daughter suddenly went from disinterested counseling client to hospital patient on a seventy-two-hour hold—an involuntary psychiatric hospital stay—when she became suicidal. Monica said,

> I knew that I didn't have what it took to help her. I found the system hard to navigate because I didn't know anything about it. You just learn as you go. I felt like I had to constantly keep my eyes and ears open and ask questions: what about this, how do we help that, what happens with this, how do we do that? You don't know the questions you need to ask so you can't ask them. It felt like a cycle where something needs to be done, I don't know what it is, but I need to keep trying to figure out what it is.

Monica discovered that, because her daughter was in a public high school, she had options for care. But she didn't know that until it was too late, because no one told her, even though the school knew of her mental health issues. Monica said, "My main frustration was everyone kept saying, 'Help her, help her, she needs more help,' but nobody could tell me where to go to get that help and how to find it so that I knew my child was safe when I put her there."

Even when someone has navigated the system and found the greatest possible care, privacy laws place serious limitations on families. Even the best professionals are bound by these laws, which are well intentioned but place serious strain on people's ability to care for their loved ones. Under current laws, family members—even spouses and parents of adult children—cannot gain access to medical information without the written consent of the person under treatment. In some states, parents must obtain written consent from children twelve and older.

To anyone who has sought treatment for a loved one in the throes of a psychotic episode, suicidal ideations or debilitating depression, this idea is laughable. It is nearly impossible to help someone in this situation understand the need to read and sign a consent form and to get that person's cooperation. Later, if treatment has restored the person to full capacity, he or she might sign consent forms. But for someone with an ongoing illness, paranoia, shame, denial of illness, resistance to care or resentment of the family's involvement, such consent may never materialize. The family is left out of the circle of treatment, and the professionals operate in a vacuum without the additional insight and history a family can bring.

My dad describes his anger at this roadblock in the system:

The psychiatrist observed my wife in a fifteen-minute appointment. I dealt with her 24/7. I felt the psychiatrist did not understand her real needs. I was angry and frustrated because I couldn't talk directly to my wife's psychiatrist or therapist about her needs. I had to get a power of attorney and show the paper to my wife's therapist before he would let me into a counseling session with my wife, even though she had invited me to come.

Someone in my dad's support group said she wrote letters to her family member's psychiatrist, letting him know what was happening at home, even though the psychiatrist couldn't respond. So Dad took this suggestion, and he and other family members have occasionally sent letters to psychiatrists and counselors, with no acknowledgment or response, in hope that the mental health professional will take notice and be enlightened.

Cheryl has experienced tremendous frustration as she's tried to help Mom without the official power to do so and without access to her medical history.

> I remember several times when Mom would be catatonic in her bed—Dad was sometimes home, sometimes at work trying not to get fired—and I would be calling place after place to see if they could take someone like Mom, describing her behavior, calling to see if the insurance would help, trying to figure out what kind of doctor would deal with something like this, trying to remember what doctors she'd seen before, trying to get all this done so I could get to work or to my next class at college. I have spoken to doctor after doctor who has tried to find ways around the privacy laws (like "hypothetical conversations") to tell/ask me information about Mom, since she was too paranoid to sign something or too catatonic to say anything.

In an extreme case, when Mom left home and our family tried for weeks to find her, we contacted every hospital and shelter in the city, and none of them could tell us if she was or had been with them. By God's provision, some family acquaintances who lived four hundred miles away traveled to the city for Thanksgiving and spent part of their holiday serving a meal to people living in one of the homeless shelters there. They recognized Mom and, through the grapevine, let us know she was living there.

As it turned out, Mom had stayed in three of the shelters we had contacted, and this most recent shelter had recognized her needs and found a place for her in the day program at one of the hospitals we had contacted. Even though we had talked with both the shelter and the hospital, because they were unable to acknowledge that she was with them, they had no information about her background, her history of mental illness or the loved ones who desperately wanted to support her treatment. Because they had spoken only with her, they didn't know she had a safe home where she could stay and a loving family who wanted to care for her. They didn't even know her full name.

My friend Marlena talked about the agony of knowing her dad needed treatment but wouldn't get it: "He had to threaten or try to kill himself or others before he could be involuntarily admitted. My father would not voluntarily admit himself into the hospital. He didn't think anything was wrong with him, only others." So the family waited until he threatened Marlena's brother and others. They also worried he'd kill himself or others while driving drunk. "We had the police make a mental health arrest—arresting him against his will. While it was difficult for us to do, we thought it necessary for his safety and the safety of others. But it took a while for him to meet the requirements for that arrest."

Short-Term Solutions

Imagine going to the doctor with chest pain, being rushed to the hospital, undergoing surgery and being sent home without being told what went wrong with your body. You'd probably continue in your previous lifestyle. Sure, they gave you some pills at the hospital, but you're better now, so you don't need to take them. Guess what. Before long you're back at the hospital again and you don't know why. And no one ever diagnoses you with anything but "chest pain." How would you possibly learn to care for yourself as you need to?

Even when families do get the necessary consent to be involved, because this system is focused on stabilization, medication and keeping people safe, it has no room for educating families and collaborating with them. So families may not understand their family members' diagnoses, the importance of medication or where they can find help from other people who have gone through the same thing.

I spoke to one woman who described her realization that the system felt no responsibility to the families of people under treatment: "At that time I finally understood the word *crazy*," she said. "Crazy was not my mother. And crazy was not this family that I lived in. Crazy was the system that didn't believe the individuals or their families could be educated."

Part of the education ill people and their families need is diagnosis. They need to understand that they're dealing with illness, what kind of treatment they can expect, why their medications are necessary and how therapy might benefit them. But the current system is reluctant to label people with diagnoses because of the stigma they might face out in the world. The diagnoses can become problematic with insurance companies as well because some consider certain illnesses "untreatable." And until recently, insurance companies have been allowed to deny coverage or to provide unequal coverage for mental health issues. So families are left guessing—or believing a three-day hospital stay has fixed the problem.

My family didn't receive confirmation of Mom's diagnosis of schizophrenia until decades after her symptoms first appeared—decades after she was first hospitalized, entered the system and started a mental health history that did not follow her from place to place. We suspected we were dealing with schizophrenia, but the initial revelation came by accident. According to Mom,

> During one of the hospitalizations, a nurse referred in conversation to "your schizophrenia." I asked her if that was true because I had never heard that stated before. The nurse said she didn't know if it was true, she just used that as a general term, and if I wanted to know I would have to ask my doctor. I asked the doctor, who said he didn't really know yet. It

could be related to schizophrenia, but he was more apt to think it was severe depression. He would need to observe me for a while before he knew for sure.

Again, this was after decades of treatment.

Another woman, who parents a son with bipolar disorder and who is herself a nurse, said, "His first doctor didn't give him a formal diagnosis because of stigma. I could shoot her for it, because we didn't know what we were dealing with. I would have been a lot more aggressive and seen to it that he stuck with the plan, except there was never really a plan. No one educated us; we didn't have a clue."

Monica talked about the constraints of dealing with insurance companies. While her daughter was in residential care, Monica spoke with her therapist on the phone and received a description of what was going on with her daughter. "Finally at one point I said, 'You know, this is much more than depression. Even someone like me can see that, and I'm just the mom.'" She discovered that professionals hesitate to diagnose anyone—especially someone under eighteen—with borderline personality disorder because some insurance companies consider the disorder untreatable and won't cover its treatment. "When I look at my daughter now," Monica says, "I don't think she would be diagnosed BPD [bipolar disorder]. With dialectical behavioral therapy, coupled with many things that she learned in residential care, I don't think she would meet the criteria now. Which to me says this is very treatable."

Speaking of insurance, cost concerns mean pressure on both doctors and patients to keep hospital stays short. People sometimes have to jump through painful hoops to get the treatment they need. For my parents' insurance company, Mom had to go through a "gatekeeper" to satisfy requirements every time she needed to receive psychiatric care. She had to share her life story for the insurance company's gatekeeper to make the right recommendation.

This was excruciating for her because she had to be extremely open about things that caused her great pain—and she wouldn't see that person for more than one session. On one occasion, an insurance representative visited Mom's hospital room and threatened her about the costs to the insurance company for her care.

The average length of a hospital stay for psychiatric care is about seven days.[2] Unfortunately, generally this is not long enough to tell whether meds are working. As one NAMI representative told me, "The average length for just an antidepressant to work is two to six weeks. So even if they start on a medicine, by the time they're discharged, we don't even know if that's the right medicine for them. So they go back to the hospital and get labeled 'frequent flyers.' They feel like they failed when really it was the medication that failed; it wasn't them."

Other people return to the hospital because it's the only way they know how to get help with their medications. Monica described the process of trying to find someone to manage her daughter's medication:

> The therapist we were seeing at the time finally said, I think you need to change meds. Well, her general practitioner wouldn't oversee that because he felt he wasn't qualified to, which I can understand. But trying to find someone else was near impossible. Psychiatrists have two- or three-month waiting periods before you can get in to see them. And in the meantime, your child is suicidal and self-harming and threatening to run away. And boy, that is a really, really broken part of the system. So one of the benefits of her being hospitalized on a seventy-two-hour hold was getting in quicker to see someone to oversee the meds. For better or worse, that's how it worked.

The hospitalization experience itself can be dehumanizing and humiliating for both patients and their families. I recently stayed one night in the hospital after surgery, and I felt like I was staying at a resort (except for the pain and the monitors beeping next to my bed all night). My surgeon was like a rock star, praised for his expertise and promoted as one of the many reasons patients should choose that hospital. All the rooms were private, the furniture was new, and I got to order my food from a room-service menu. Have you visited the psychiatric wing of a hospital? It doesn't look like the wing where they perform knee replacements and heart surgeries. And when was the last time you saw a hospital advertise its world-renowned psychiatrists in an effort to attract patients?

I didn't visit the psychiatric wing of the hospital where I stayed, but if it's typical, it's probably in the basement or in the older part of the building, and it probably contains the furniture they cleared out of my room to make way for the new. Psychiatry, the medical practice of psychology, doesn't have the prestige of other kinds of medical practice. And because of its focus on stabilizing, medicating and keeping people safe, its spaces are generally built to accomplish only those three things, not to keep people comfortable or to help them feel respected.

One woman talked about going to the hospital with her mom when she was admitted for psychiatric care. She describes the sense of humiliation:

> You know, when you walk into a locked unit and that door clicks closed, it's got this piercing sound to it. And I always know when I hear that sound, it means you're not getting out of there unless somebody lets you out.
>
> As my mom went through the admission process, they asked her, "Do you have any sharp objects?" They went through her purse, looking for anything sharp. They asked her to take off her belt and her shoelaces because they were concerned about suicidal risk. And there were two nurses in

the background, behind a desk, who were laughing. I'm not even saying that they were laughing at my mom, but I was an adolescent, not saying anything but observing everybody. And all I ever wanted somebody to say was that they were going to take good care of my mom.

The Last Stop

Among those who refuse hospitalization, reject medication, don't respond well to treatment or simply fall through the cracks, many end up in circumstances much more dehumanizing and humiliating than hospitalization: life on the streets or in prison.

Just as it is almost impossible to force treatment on someone legally, it's not possible to force anyone to come in off the street. So some families have to live with the reality that someone they love is spending days and nights out on the street or in barely adequate shelters, exposed to the worst elements of the environment and of human nature. Determining demographics of the homeless population is difficult for obvious reasons, and a variety of statistics are reported, but most reliable sources report that about 40 percent of homeless people have some kind of mental health problem, and 20 to 25 percent of homeless people have serious mental illness.[3]

Even though we can't force a person to seek treatment, the legal system can—and this is what may happen if a person with mental illness breaks the law. It's a dirty little secret: incarceration serves as a net to catch many people who need help and should have received it long before they ended up in front of a judge. Again, statistics vary, but the Department of Justice itself estimates that in the United States, more than half of inmates have symptoms of serious mental illness—ranging from 45 percent of inmates in federal prisoners to 56 percent in state prisoners and 64 percent in local jails.[4] The National Alliance on Mental Illness (NAMI) says this statistic means "the mental healthcare system is failing—long before people enter the criminal justice system and after they leave it. Individuals are sentenced to lives without hope and enormous costs shifted on to our police, courts, jails and prisons at all levels."[5]

So for some people, jail is a default treatment center and police are the mental health workers. Officers may or may not know what to do with a mentally ill person, but for better or worse, they're often the only option.

The positive side is that once a person enters the legal system, if a mental illness is present and demonstrated, he or she can be compelled to receive treatment. This may actually serve as the means for someone to get better. This was the case for Mom, who was stabilized on medications during her prison sentence and has maintained consistency with her meds since then.

Unfortunately, prison is a tough place to receive mental health care—or any kind of care. It's a tough place for a healthy person to cope, let alone a person who is seriously ill. And the structure and regulations of the prison system are built for people who are healthy. When Mom was in prison, I wanted to visit her. But I couldn't just stop by for a visit; I had to apply for acceptance as an approved visitor. And the process defeated me.

In this process, the inmate had to initiate the desire for visitors by requesting that a form from the prison be mailed to anyone she wanted to receive as a visitor. When the forms made their way to potential visitors, they had to fill them out and mail them back for approval. After officials completed their checks and granted approval, they notified the inmate, who then had the responsibility to notify the visitors that they had been approved. For Mom, this process was impossible. So I never visited.

Coping Mechanisms

So, how do families cope with all this trouble? They find ways—some healthy, some not. God has made people remarkably resilient. One of the ways we maintain our resiliency is by employing coping mechanisms to help us through times of crisis. These mechanisms help us function when we must shut down nonessential thought processes and emotions. They protect our inner selves from serious damage when reality becomes too much to handle. These mechanisms are a blessing in a short-term crisis.

But in cases of serious and chronic illness like schizophrenia, family members develop long-term coping mechanisms that may help them in the short term but aren't always healthy— "emergency measures" that aren't meant for long-term use. For example, people use denial to protect themselves emotionally as they adjust to a new and difficult reality. After that adjustment happens, denial is no longer useful but harmful. Other people escape into a fantasy world that provides much-needed relief but over time diminishes their capacity to function in the real world.

These mechanisms can help us survive. But they can also enslave us when they become long-term habits and we forget how to function without them. This is one of the things that happens when people lack the safety and stability of a healthy family.

In my family, we all developed our own ways of coping with my mother's illness. I emotionally and mentally compartmentalized my home life and life outside it so that I literally could be one person at home and another everywhere else. When I wasn't at home, I didn't give much thought to my mother's illness or our family's troubles. And I didn't talk about my family life with anyone; not even my best friend knew about my mother's struggle.

I remember hearing other teenage girls complain about fights with their moms and wishing I could fight with my mom because it seemed so normal—and my mom would have to be strong to fight with me. So in conversation with my friends, I sometimes made up a story about a fight that never could have happened. When I was home, I tried desperately to help and fix my mother and to suppress my negative emotions, which I didn't know how to handle. Unfortunately, this had the long-term effect of distancing me from all my emotions—including positive ones—which I have since had to painstakingly learn to embrace and which I continue to struggle to express.

My brother also talks about using distance to cope: "My tendency is to respond to my mother's illness by withdrawing myself from it, ignoring it as much as possible and avoiding further pain by not facing up to it."

Kate talked about how she coped as a child: "When Mom came back from the hospital, my coping mechanism was denial and minimizing contact with her. I also related to her as if she were a child. I remember trying to teach her about life philosophies and feeling like she didn't know any of it."

She also talked about how she continues to cope as an adult "by creating a false image of what my mother is and was like":

> It is based on reality, but leaves out much of reality. I think this allows me to feel a little more normal and to identify with her more. I don't know if this coping mechanism is a product or a tool, but I also use it to deal with other difficult people in my life. I focus on the characteristics I want and discard the ones I don't.

One pastor I spoke with talked about the denial he sees among families in his congregation: "They say, 'We don't want to deal with this. We don't want to talk about this. They'll be okay.' It's interesting—you can hardly sit still and there's a new medication out. And yet every time somebody gets a prescription, they don't want to fill it because that means something is wrong."

Monica tried various distractions: "I spent a lot of time spinning my wheels, doing research and immersing myself in that, or staying up late and distracting myself with mindless computer or TV or whatever."

Everyone in crisis uses coping mechanisms for a variety of reasons. One is simply to ensure survival. In the case of mental illness, another reason is to avoid shame. Even though mental illness is common, suffering people feel an inherent danger and lack of openness in the world around them—including in the church. So they feel the need to protect themselves not only from the emotional wounds of the illness itself, but also from blows inflicted by insensitive people. These blows should not come from fellow Christians, but sadly they do.

So are you feeling overwhelmed? Wishing you hadn't read this and the previous chapter? Wondering what you can possibly do? This truth is painful, isn't it? It's critical for churches to understand the experiences of suffering people and their families so they understand how to come alongside them.

These are real people—25 percent of our population and everyone who loves them. They deserve better. We can't change everything about the suffering of mental illness and its treatment. We can't take mental illness away. But we can do better in the church. We can extend the humanizing, loving friendship every hurting person needs.

CHURCH LIFE

Dad was a pastor for ten years. He ministered to two congregations and left the second church before Mom's illness manifested itself in full psychosis. However, as I mentioned earlier, she did struggle with some symptoms of mental illness throughout her adult life, including during the years when Dad was in pastoral ministry.

While Dad didn't recognize the true nature of Mom's difficulties at first, her ongoing struggle with mental health meant that he sometimes had to spend extra time at home, either caring for her or helping care for the rest of the family. He saw this as simply living up to biblical priorities, but it was something he had to explain to the churches that employed him. Dad remembers, "When I took responsibilities of pastoring a church, I wanted them to be aware that my first responsibility was to God, my second responsibility was to my family, and then my third responsibility was to the church." At times his responsibility to his family created "tensions between the church and the family," and members of the congregation were not always understanding about the impact on his ministry to the church.

After leaving the second church, Dad never served as a full-time pastor again. He did fill in as preacher while pastors were away from their churches, and he served as an interim pastor for a time. But, he says, "there was a time when I felt like I could not do it anymore. My time, my energies were needed here at home. I felt the Lord had something more important for me to do." So my family settled into membership in our local church as laypeople.

In general, my parents have felt supported as laypeople in the church because they have connected with a few people who have been tremendously encouraging and who have prayed for them and walked with them through ugly times. One couple in their church, John and Peggy, visited Mom a few times while she was in the county jail and attended court hearings with Dad. Dad says, "Their presence made me feel like I was not alone." Peggy, who is a professional counselor, made herself available to listen to Dad each Sunday morning at church and once visited with Mom by phone in the middle of the night to help her process her thoughts.

A few other people in the church made themselves available to drive Mom to appointments when Dad was working and unable to take her. Some of the men in the church listened to Dad as he shared his needs with them. "What an encouragement it was to talk to someone willing to listen and understand," he recalls. My parents are gracious people for whom a little encouragement goes a long way.

But most people, including pastors, have kept their distance from both Mom and Dad. In Dad's experience, most people in the church have been "a little fearful to talk to me or didn't know what to say, or just fearful of mental illness in general. And it was basically just a few people who were comfortable talking with me, and I would feel kind of left out in relationships."

As for my siblings and me, no one offered us extra support or asked what we might need. It just never came up. My sisters and I were active in the youth group and other church activities; no one asked how we were doing or how things were at home.

NEARLY HALF (44.5 PERCENT) of church leaders are approached two to five times per year for help in dealing with mental illness; 32.8 percent are approached more frequently, from six to more than twelve times per year.

I mentioned a couple of times that my mom was sick or in the hospital, but no one followed up to find out more about what was going on. I had the sense that people knew what was going on and didn't want to acknowledge it—which may or may not be true. I also got the message that more information would not be welcome, and I should be ashamed and keep my mouth shut. I got pretty good at compartmentalizing and acting at church as if everything were normal and fine.

Cheryl says,

One time the church gave us a check from the benevolence fund to help financially. Another time the pastor saw me walk out of a Sunday school class crying, and he told me something like that he cared that things were hard. These things were helpful, but I remember no other acknowledgments or sympathetic offerings. I don't think anyone would have known what to do or what was really wrong. So when we were able to participate on a normal level, we fit in. When we couldn't, we stayed quiet. The church we attended was full of people who seemed to me to have everything together as a requirement to attend, so I pretended that we did too.

Kate felt the same sense of shame I did, especially the first time Mom was hospitalized and a few people from the church brought us meals. For her, there was some relief in the silence:

I remember being at first terrified that people at church may know. I remember watching to see who had brought us food and hoping that it wouldn't be the kids I didn't want to know. I have no recollection of anyone at church ever speaking to me about my mother's illness. It was completely brushed aside, but at the same time I was happy with that, because then I could continue to pretend to be normal.

I believe the church was as confused as we were, and the people in our church were responding the best way they knew how. But the silence wasn't healthy for us or for them. And when the church is silent to a person in crisis, it can sound remarkably like silence from God.

Struggling in the Church

Christians should understand what people with mental illness and their families are experiencing within the walls of the church. On top of the general troubles I outlined in chapter three, people in the church experience a new set of difficulties in a place they probably came to seeking a spiritual lifeline and healing. Among people who have carried their own mental health struggles or family members' struggles into the church, some common themes emerge.

Stigma. This is big. Our culture—including the church—stigmatizes mental illness to a degree that it now stigmatizes almost nothing else. This stigma is deeply ingrained in our thinking about people with mental illness, and it is at the root of much of what I discuss in the rest of this chapter. I've devoted an entire chapter to it (chapter seven), so you'll soon have the opportunity to read about it in more detail. I mention it here because it is important to acknowledge in a discussion of what people experience in the church.

People with mental illness and their families run up against a stigma that means immediate, mindless, irrational rejection because they are "tainted" by mental illness. They are marked for shame. They are labeled, stereotyped, misunderstood and dismissed.

One pastor I talked with said it this way: "The church has done a disservice to those struggling with mental health, because they have stigmatized it, and they just don't want to deal with it; they don't want to take an honest look at it."

Another pastor, who also had a professional career as a social worker, gave an extreme example from a church she had been part of. The church split after church leaders developed a practice of inexpertly "diagnosing" people in the church with mental illnesses, labeling them and driving them out. These nonprofessionals felt they could diagnose mental disorders, and the diagnoses themselves served as justification for getting people out of the church.

Marlena describes the reaction of her father's church after his illness became apparent: "He was a pariah. I am sure people couldn't distinguish between a malevolent criminal and someone who was mentally ill."

WHEN CHURCH PEOPLE are on medication or diagnosed with a mental illness, they generally keep the matter very private (33.7 percent) within the church or share the information with only a few trusted friends (37.6 percent). Only 12.5 percent of respondents said the matter is openly talked about in a healthy way.

A father I talked with said this about his son: "He would go the ninetieth mile not to expose himself as bipolar. Because then, all of a sudden, all of people's caricatures come into play. And they start to wonder, *Oh, are you going to, like, start jumping up and down and go crazy? Dress up like a clown and chase me with a knife?* That creates loneliness and needs to be exposed. You need to speak it; you need to talk about it."

Monica told me about how her daughter's illness affected her church life:

> I could probably count on one hand the number of people I shared that with—just because of stigma, because as a Christian parent your kids aren't supposed to do those things. I felt like I would have to really defend myself, and I was in no state to do that. So it was easier to just not display it or just not make it known so that I wouldn't have to defend it. Now I have met other people at church who have very specific diagnoses, and we've kind of shared those things, but it's hidden, it's kind of hushed, it's not very out there.

Another friend told me, "I can't say the church did anything right or wrong, because I never gave anyone a chance to respond to my situation. I kept it all inside out of shame." Openly acknowledging a mental illness means opening yourself for others to project their stereotypes onto you. It means some people will stop thinking of you as a person like them and think of you only as needy, unstable or dangerous. Or as a lost cause, a wasted life. It means feeling others' unwarranted rejection, a new distance between you and other people, and the sense that they assume you should be ashamed of yourself—even though they can't explain why. The stigma, more than anything, causes people to be terrified of acknowledging and seeking help for mental illnesses and disorders.

The pretenders. I've mentioned this several times already: the pressure to pretend everything is fine. I felt it not only in the church but also at school and elsewhere. But the church may be the place where dropping the façade would have done the most good. It's harder to feel accepted by Christ and covered by his grace when you're hiding in the church.

Angie talks about her experience growing up in the church:

> I thought I was not being a good enough Christian. My church was an authority, and the ethos was that Christians

don't have problems. I felt like I had to put on a certain persona when I was there. That feeling, recognition of that hypocrisy, almost drove me away from God completely. I just kind of rebelled against the church for a while. It really was not a safe place; you couldn't be real.

One of the pastors I spoke with recognized this problem in many churches: "If we're coming to church, there's got to be a certain image, we've got to put on a certain façade. So we have marginalized those who appear different."

People in mental health crisis, as with any other crisis, need friends. They need connection with loving people—especially those who will point them to Christ. And this kind of loving connection is impossible in an environment that asks people to make the rest of us more comfortable by pretending to be healthy, happy and impervious to trouble.

No mess allowed. Like everything else we touch, the church is an imperfect institution. It's full of imperfect, self-obsessed, self-protective people like you and me. It doesn't come naturally for us to develop deep, selfless relationships with the people we shake hands with once a week on Sunday. And in a hectic and transient world like ours, it's no wonder we often bounce off each other on our way to somewhere else.

Dwight L. Carlson says in his book *Why Do Christians Shoot Their Wounded?*, "Most churches have their measures of 'success': a certain number of converts, a specified increase in 'giving units,' a 'star' pastor or youth leader, an array of flashy programs, or the numerical growth of the congregation. When we focus on these external things, however, all too often we neglect and inadvertently hurt the wounded among us."[1]

In this environment, people have little tolerance for sticky messes—the kind that really are ugly, that stink, that stick to you and won't completely wash off. These messes slow us down and require us to wrestle with questions we'd rather avoid (for more on some of these questions, see chapter seven). Mental illness is exactly this kind of mess; ministering to people with mental illness requires us to get closer to them than—let's be honest—many of us would like to get.

Christians don't suffer. In her book *Darkness Is My Only Companion*, Kathryn Greene-McCreight shares journal entries, stories and spiritual insights from her experience living with bipolar disorder. She mentions this about Christians' response to mental illness: "Christian communities still have a fear of the mentally ill. In part they do not understand mental illness, in part there is a false assumption that the Christian life should always be an easy path, and in part the problem of suffering is hard to grasp."[2]

OF SURVEY RESPONDENTS, 29.1 percent said that, on average, mental illness is never mentioned in sermons at their church; 20.6 percent said mental illness is mentioned once a year; and 29.4 percent two to three times per year.

In many churches, intentionally or unintentionally, the overriding emphasis is on "victorious Christian living," with the basic assumption that real Christians don't have problems—or at least not crippling, persistent problems that a prayer or two won't cure. Some churches purposely embrace this as a basic doctrine. Many more churches adopt it without realizing they've done so. This theology is based on the belief that as Christians we should expect complete victory over the effects of sin here and now—as evidence of our faith and God's love for us.

This is in direct contradiction to what Jesus said: "Here on earth you will have many trials and sorrows. But take heart, because I have overcome the world" (Jn 16:33). Peter said we shouldn't be surprised when Christians suffer, not just in spite of their faith but *because of it:* "Dear friends, don't be surprised at the fiery trials you are going through, as if something strange were happening to you. Instead, be very glad—for these trials make you partners with Christ in his suffering, so that you will have the wonderful joy of seeing his glory when it is revealed to all the world" (1 Pet 4:12-13).

James anticipated trouble for Christians and called us to "consider it an opportunity for great joy" (Jas 1:2). Paul wrote of "a thorn in my flesh, a messenger from Satan to torment me and keep me from becoming proud." And when he begged God to take it away, the Lord did not remove it but assured him: "My power works best in weakness" (2 Cor 12:7-9). God doesn't only allow our suffering; he appreciates it for his own sake.

The writer of Hebrews dedicated a portion of the book to memorializing the faith of God's people throughout history, demonstrating how their faith had pleased God and drawn them toward a future promise of blessing they could not see. This writer described the way these faithful people

> were tortured, refusing to turn from God in order to be set free. They placed their hope in a better life after the resurrection. Some were jeered at, and their backs were cut open with whips. Others were chained in prisons. Some died by stoning, some were sawed in half, and others were killed with the sword. Some went about wearing skins of sheep and goats, destitute and oppressed and mistreated. They were too good for this world, wandering over deserts and mountains, hiding in caves and holes in the ground. All these people earned a good reputation because of their faith, yet none of them received all that God had promised. (Heb 11:35-39)

If these saints suffered so bitterly, why should we not suffer? If their faith in the promise of Christ did not exempt them from suffering—in fact, was the cause of mistreatment and abuse—why should we expect an easy life?

This idea that Christians don't suffer is also in direct contradiction to the actual experience of true Christians, all of whom slug their way through trouble daily and find themselves at the mercy of decay, pain and sorrow—such as that brought on by a mental illness or disorder. When churches emphasize victory in a way that suggests Christians don't experience problems, they alienate and undermine the faith of suffering people of all kinds, including those touched by mental illness.

My friend Angie remembers her church sending this message as she was growing up: "Everything was just victorious Christian living. . . . Nothing about mental illness at all. I remember one woman in the church saying what a bad person this counselor was because he was encouraging people to look at their problems and that's not a Christian way of doing things."

Monica talked about finally coming to a realization: "It's okay to not have answers and it's okay to wrestle with my questions and it's okay to even think those questions; whereas before I thought, *Oh no, I can't do that, I'm a Christian, I'm not allowed.* There has been great freedom in knowing that God lets me wrestle with him and that's okay. I think that God really welcomes that."

I don't want to suggest that it's inappropriate to talk about spiritual victory. We do have victory in Christ. As forgiven people, we are no longer slaves to sin and its ultimate consequence: "We know that our old sinful selves were crucified with Christ so that sin might lose its power in our lives. We are no longer slaves to sin" (Rom 6:6). But while we are not slaves, we still live in the slaves' quarters. Our world is poisoned by sin, our bodies are cursed, and all of our endeavors are flawed. God has promised to remove us from this world someday and to replace these imperfect bodies with new bodies (including, I believe, new brains) suited for life in a perfect world without decay. We can walk in the light of that future hope, even though we live in a shadowy world. When churches embrace this dual reality, they help bring lifesaving hope to suffering people.

Spiritualizing the problem. Even among churches that do acknowledge that Christians have problems, for some reason many have a hard time accepting that mental illness is not simply a spiritual problem. Perhaps because brain disorders affect a person's cognitive abilities and emotional processing, and therefore spiritual expression, many Christians are deeply confused about what causes mental illness. Many assume it is caused by demon possession or demonic attack. Others believe it can be cured by more faith or that it's caused by unconfessed sin.

As one woman put it, "The first thing about church was, if you've got a problem, you must not be walking with the Lord." Another woman, who was affected by depression and sought counseling, was told by her pastor that she must have undealt-with sin in her life that was causing her depression.

I believe our minds, bodies and spirits are more interrelated than we can understand. And we know that each of these elements of who we are can have a powerful effect on the others. I won't deny that spiritual problems can lead to problems in our brains and bodies, just as physical suffering can affect our spirits. But this does not justify the assumption that all mental illness is spiritual at its root and can be cured through more spiritual work on our part—any more than we should expect to cure cancer by simply confessing sin and praying more.

Spiritualizing mental illness translates to blaming sick people for their illnesses. It also means that family members of people with mental illness also get the message that their sin and lack of faith may be the problem. It traps people into working harder and harder to achieve a level of righteousness that will justify their freedom from illness. This is not the gospel message, and it is very effective in discouraging people from acknowledging their struggles and seeking help.

No such thing. Here's another big issue: many Christians, including some pastors and other church leaders, deny there is such a thing as mental illness. This is closely related to spiritualizing the problem, but it goes beyond assuming the problem has spiritual origins and claims that no illness exists. A full analysis of this viewpoint is best left for another book (and probably another author), but I will say I believe the Christian suspicion of mental illness and mental health care is rooted in the same cultural stigma that causes us to view mental illness as a socially unacceptable form of illness, unique in its origins and cures, that ends a person's hopes for meaningful life or productive contribution.

One woman I spoke with, who works for the National Alliance on Mental Illness, said this about her work to support churches: "However the pastor thinks, so goes the congregation. I think of one pastor whose daughter was self-injuring, and he felt like she just needed more biblical counseling. When another person disclosed their illness, the elders wanted to exorcise demons."

I find it ironic that when people claim there's no such thing as physical illness—that it is simply an illusion caused by faulty beliefs—orthodox Christian believers reject such claims as heresy and the teaching of cults. Yet when people deny that illnesses and disorders can attack the brain and warp our thoughts and feelings, their claims are generally received and respected within our ranks. We are horrified by people whose religious beliefs cause them to deny treatment to the sick and dying, and yet it's acceptable for Christians to claim that mental illnesses should not be treated, because such treatments are not described in the Bible. The Bible does not describe the use of chemotherapy, painkillers or general anesthesia either.

I recently read an article by a Christian writer questioning whether Christians should take antidepressants, because emotional pain can cause us to lean more heavily on Christ. Physical pain can have the same effect, but when I had back surgery, no one questioned whether I should allow the surgeon to use general anesthesia. And no one condemned me for taking pain medication for several weeks afterward while I worked toward healing. Yes, severe emotional pain and other symptoms of mental illness can drive us closer to our Savior. They can also drive us to cause serious harm to the people around us, reject our faith, believe lies and commit suicide.

I can't imagine anyone holding to this view if they have loved a person stricken with serious mental illness and then seen that person's life saved and faith restored through medical intervention and counseling. Denying the reality of mental illness has the same effect as denying the reality of other illness: it discourages treatment and stands in the way of redemption. It hinders agonized people from crying out in their pain, bringing their illness to Jesus and finding ease for their suffering. It forces sick people and their loved ones to choose between the church and life.

Uninformed clergy. When a mental illness becomes apparent and even when it's diagnosed by a professional, many people don't know where to turn for help. Because the system is so difficult to navigate, people with mental illness and their loved ones often turn to the church for either help in dealing with illness or simply direction in finding treatment and support. For most pastors, training in mental health extends to prayer and referral. For some pastors and other church leaders, it doesn't extend even that far. So when people come to them for help, they may not be able to offer much direction. Or they may simply refer the person to a counselor and consider their job done. And the person seeking help is caught in the headlights of a daunting system without a spiritual guide.

I asked one psychiatrist and one counselor about their experiences in consulting with church leaders. The psychiatrist has been in his church for twenty-five years, has served as a deacon and currently serves as an elder. The counselor has been on pastoral staffs and is engaged in youth ministry and other ministries in the church. Both of these men have decades of professional experience behind them, and both said they have never had a pastor or other church leader consult them for help or education in understanding mental illness. They have had people in the church—including church leaders—informally ask for referrals or advice in dealing with a specific person or situation (the psychiatrist called these "curbside consults") but never formal equipment or education.

Like it or not, the church serves as a triage center for many people with mental illness. In crisis, it's only natural to turn first to a known and trusted friend, and people expect the church to be a friend like that. Pastors should know when to refer people to mental health professionals for help, but when they don't recognize their own needs for some basic education as well, they're likely to let people down as they're walking through darkness.

Condemnation. People with mental illness and their families—especially parents of children with mental illness—often feel condemned for their suffering. Instead of walking through the doors of the church to find the no-condemnation grace of Jesus, they find an assumption that they must have done something to deserve their suffering. They find a subtle expectation that they'd better fix themselves if they want to be part of the fellowship. And, again, they face a viewpoint that people who struggle with mental illness are beyond hope until they get their act together.

Monica, who was divorced after her first husband abandoned his family and widowed when her second husband died, feared the church's condemnation when her daughter was diagnosed with mental illness. She said, "There are those who will step in with you and walk with you, but I think they are more the exception than the rule. Especially as a parent having been divorced and having been widowed, I felt a fear of condemnation. I mean, I condemned myself enough."

My brother-in-law Kevin, struggling with serious depression

and thoughts of suicide, was introduced to the church as a teenager and was immediately alienated by condemnation for his depression. He said,

> It was at the end of seventh grade when I had a better idea about what was wrong with me. My brother had friends who were attending a youth group, and he invited me. On the night I decided to go, they were speaking about peer pressure and other teen things. Then the youth pastor brought up suicide and depression. My skin crawled, and I felt uncomfortable. The youth pastor said that suicide and depression were the work of Satan and that everyday people can be encouraged by Satan to hurt God and themselves.
>
> My brother and his friends ran about playing games, and I contemplated if what I had done and felt in my past was going to condemn me. I had never felt so guilty in my life before this. I had trouble sleeping for days. I thought I was a Christian, but I had no idea what Jesus had done for me or the real reason he came.

Kevin eventually did learn the truth about who Jesus is and why he came to earth, and he became a follower of Jesus. His depression didn't go away at that moment, and neither did the sense of condemnation he felt from the church, even though he found hope and meaning in Christ.

Silence. Nearly everyone I've spoken with has referred to the church's deafening silence on mental illness. I believe this is rooted in stigmatization as well. Because we believe mental illness is shameful and dooms a person to a life that's not worth living, we are reluctant to even mention it (unless we're making jokes about it) in polite conversation—let alone in our sermons, Sunday school classes and public prayers. So we simply don't say anything.

Angie remembers the silence: "I can't remember any time mental illness was talked about in youth group or anything. And looking back, there were other kids . . . there were more families with issues."

Another woman, whose mother was mentally ill, said this about growing up in the church: "We always heard prayers for people who were sick, but my mom's name was never on there. I never saw anything advertised as a support group, never heard anybody talk about anything. So quite frankly, the silence in my house was just as silent in the church."

The church's silence was painful for me, and as I was growing up, this damaged my ability to believe that God could know the worst about us and still love us. My conversations with other people made clear that this is true for many people. The church's silence reinforces the stigma, reinforces the idea that mental illness is shameful. It perpetuates misunderstanding and misinformation. It marginalizes people who need ministry, and it strengthens their sense that they are suffering alone.

Impatience. For serious and chronic mental illness, there is no cure—short of a miracle. There is no "all better." Even when well managed, such illness is a lifelong reality, and relapses can happen without warning. Even for episodic illness, the road to health can be long and mountainous. Walking alongside someone with mental illness may mean a lifelong hike over peaks and valleys, learning to grow in faith and in relationship with Jesus through an illness that clouds the view. That walk might cause mistrust of reality and of a person's own thoughts. It might require extra patience for processing truth. It might repeatedly tax the resources of the church and its fellowship. And churches, like other organizations, grow tired of such taxation. Culturally, we expect people who fall down to pull themselves back up and put their hands to the plow. Sure, everyone stumbles occasionally. And we're willing to give help in times of crisis. But when the time of crisis doesn't seem to end, we start to wonder why we're still helping. Why we're not seeing progress. Why we're not moving on.

The father of a son with bipolar disorder spoke passionately from his experience:

> Attitudes have to change. This doesn't go away. That is one of the great challenges for families and for the church. Say you get hurt or you have surgery. So you're laid up, and people rally around you and give your family food and maybe take your kids out to a ballgame or something like that. Now, if they were still doing this a year from now, they'd be thinking, "Now, wait a minute, you've got to be getting better. I mean, we love you, but . . . "
>
> Well, that's the issue that anyone with mental illness or anyone who is going to minister to mental illness is going to eventually wade into. Wait a minute. We helped you with this a year ago, two years ago. The problem is like telling a diabetic, "We helped you with your blood glucose a year ago." Yeah, but guess what. They've got to do this every minute of the day until they die. So that is a daunting task, and it doesn't fall to an individual eventually—it has to fall to the whole body of Christ because it's only the body that can handle something like that for a lifetime.

A pastor said this:

> We don't have a lot of endurance to walk with people who struggle with mental illness. Some churches are really good at the short-term fix. But I really don't think we know how to walk with people who, for example, have been traumatized by a life event, and maybe they develop full-blown PTSD. We're really good at being there when the event first happens, bringing some blankets, bringing food, providing some money so people can transition, but then it's like a year later, and we ask, "You're still thinking about that?"

Kevin said this about attending church after he was hospitalized for the first time with depression:

I attended church that week with Dad and felt very uncomfortable because it felt like I was on show. I was all better now.
The pastor met us at the door and gave me a handshake then
a hug, and church began. He began the sermon with rejoicing
that I was okay, and I sank into myself even more. No one
would mention anything to me, I was defiant in asking for
help, and things just stayed the same. I was embarrassed to
ask for counsel, and they were too busy for me.

I spoke with a pastor who had a high degree of confidence that
his church was doing well in serving people with mental illness.
And relatively speaking, his church is. They have created an atmosphere where it's all right to acknowledge that people aren't perfect
and it's normal to have problems. At the same time, I heard a typical
impatience reflected in what he said to me: "My personal philosophy is that you can come here and be screwed up, you just
can't stay screwed up. We all need recovery from something." I
appreciate his emphasis on growing as a person, rather than staying
stuck. I appreciate the idea that we need to strive for sanctification
and holiness. And people with mental illness need to work hard to
manage their illnesses as effectively as possible. But they might still
"stay screwed up" over the long term, even after working hard and
taking required medications.

When churches have antibiotic-like expectations for mental
health treatment, they communicate, "Go get treated, then you can
come back and you can be a growing Christian with us." The
problem is, many people can get treated for the rest of their lives
and learn to manage an illness, but will never be "over it." For
some, their illness is a disability that will hinder them to some
degree at least occasionally and even daily. Our expectations of
healing cause frustration for everyone. And they send the false
message that God is patient and loving with us only to a point, and
past that point, we're on our own.

Out of place. In one sense, the church is full of misfits. As flawed, sinful people, none of us will ever be truly whole this side of heaven. And because our collective sin erects barriers between us, none of us consistently feels completely and truly loved, accepted and at home. Yet in most churches, just about everyone seems to have a place. We have groups and special ministries for women, men, children, teenagers, preteens, singles, parents of young children, parents of teenagers, single parents, blended families, divorced people, newlyweds. We make accommodations for those who are physically disabled or developmentally disabled; we reach out to addicts of all kinds, sex-industry workers, immigrants, nursing-home residents, people dealing with chronic pain and people in prison.

Yet I have never been to a church with a ministry specifically for people with mental illness and their loved ones. And in my research, I came across only a handful of such programs in churches in the United States. This proliferation of churches that conspicuously neglects people affected by mental illness—and, let's face it, most of the population is affected in some way—sends the message "You don't belong. You're the only one like you here." It also sends the message that mental health issues are beyond the realm of the church's interest and care.

Message received.

Sure, churches feel unqualified to help people manage and treat mental illness. And except for those church members who are professionally qualified, they should feel this way. They should recognize their limitations. But last time I checked, churches as a whole were also not qualified to help developmentally disabled people improve their motor skills, help people manage chronic pain or teach addicts to overcome their addictions—and yet many churches don't think twice about supporting people with these needs. No professional qualifications are required to be a friend.

On the flip side, many people with mental illness would like to do ministry in the church but aren't sure whether they are allowed. In some churches they may be specifically told no; in other churches this question may be handled on a case-by-case basis or may not be addressed at all. In many churches, the emphasis on quality of service, production value in worship and qualifications leads people to believe they're not qualified to minister to others because they may not always be able to bring their best selves to church. That leaves only the option to be recipients of ministry, usually without any ministry setting where their needs are addressed.

One friend, who suffered with an anxiety disorder, told me, "Anxiety affected my life at church to the extent that I was too afraid to volunteer for anything. I dreaded speaking in public because I *always* got a panic attack in this situation. Although I longed to lead a Bible study or small group, fear kept me from jumping in for years."

One counselor told me that, in her experience with clients,

one of the things people really want to do when they have a church home is to find their niche: Where do I belong within this body of believers? Is it in a small-group setting, a ministry setting or both? Is it nowhere? Sometimes people feel like they shouldn't volunteer for a position because they might go through a period of time where they're really not going to be effective or efficient. So they don't necessarily feel comfortable putting themselves out there. Finding that niche is a challenge for a lot of people, but once they find it, it's great. It works really well. They find their niche because they feel comfortable with someone.

In doing research for this book, I found it interesting that when I asked people whether they were aware of any churches doing a good job of ministering to people with mental illness, they repeatedly mentioned churches that have strong, intentional ministries to children with developmental disabilities like Down syndrome and cerebral palsy. These are important ministries for people who themselves have suffered from stigmatization. And that stigma is fading, thanks in part to such church ministries. But to suggest that these ministries are meeting the needs of people with mental illness—such as adults with depression, anxiety disorders and bipolar disorder—is ridiculous.

Another common answer—this from pastors—was that churches have a place for people with mental illness in their recovery groups. But recovery ministries are not right for most people with mental illness. The idea of recovery reinforces the message that we want to help you "get over" your problem so you can be a normal, fully functioning member of the community, rather than a drain. This approach is appropriate for issues that truly lend themselves to recovery, but it's not appropriate for most mental illness. A person might recover from an episode of short-term depression, but people don't typically recover from bipolar disorder or schizophrenia. Someone who needs to learn to manage an ongoing disorder will not draw much benefit from sitting through a twelve-step program, life skills training for people with developmental disabilities or a support group for people healing from divorce. So people with mental illness and their families find their own place—often at the fringes of our churches.

Spiritual confusion. For people with any kind of brain disorder, accurately understanding the world can be difficult at times. Accurately understanding deep spiritual truths can be, on occasion, impossible. For people with psychosis, like my mother, mysterious spiritual matters may become fodder for complex delusions. For people with personality disorders, the concept of personal sin and repentance may be hard to fathom. Those suffering with mood and anxiety disorders may be momentarily unable to grasp the truth about God's love and grace. This is a serious challenge not only for people suffering from mental illness, but also for those who learn from them—such as their children.

My mom is a devoted follower of Christ who took a serious and destructive detour on her journey, thanks to the delusions she experienced at church. But even before that time, there was a certain level of misunderstanding and superstition (such as her belief that our clothes dryer was possessed by demons) in her spiritual life. Because I learned a lot from her growing up, I had to sort through some of these beliefs and decide to reject the ones that didn't seem to jibe with Scripture. And after I became an adult, I had to unlearn and relearn some biblical truths.

I spoke with a psychologist who gave another example. He worked with a client who had posttraumatic stress disorder. Her mother was mentally ill, and when the client was young, her mother talked with her about end-of-the-world scenarios, sharing what she believed was a special vision. Now an adult, this woman is very hesitant to have any involvement with the church because of the terror she feels when people talk about Jesus' return. The psychologist worked with her to try to separate healthy faith from what had scared her as a young child. In the meantime, this woman had passed along some spiritual misunderstandings to her own child.

It's important for church leaders to understand that people in the throes of mental illness—even illness as common as depression and anxiety disorders—may interpret biblical truth erroneously as a factor of the illness. They may think superstitiously about Jesus and his power at work in and through them; they may believe they're called to do or say something unbiblical. They may see visions or hear voices at church that prompt them to behave strangely. They may feel afraid to come to church or to get too involved. They may simply feel too worthless for God's love or too anxious to trust him.

Lack of Christian resources. When a mental health crisis hits, Christians seeking care from other Christians may be surprised at how difficult such care can be to find. Most communities have

Christian counseling practices somewhere in the area, and people might find referrals through organizations such as the American Association of Christian Counselors. But for more extensive care—residential, inpatient or outpatient care for long-term treatment—they're largely on their own.

Because there is no well-known national, nondenominational parachurch organization providing Christian mental health care, advocacy and referrals, Christian facilities can be hard to find. There is no household name that comes to mind as a place where they can turn. Again, many people are likely to turn to the church at that point, and most church leaders don't have this kind of information either, beyond the names of a few local Christian counselors. Even when someone manages to find such facilities, they may not treat the specific issue for which the person needs care.

Monica had this experience when her daughter was in crisis. "One of my frustrations in trying to find residential care for my daughter was that there are no Christian facilities that serve what she needed. There were a few Christian facilities who said, 'No, we don't take clients like that.' I was afraid for my daughter, afraid for her faith and in fear for her life." Monica did find care for her daughter, but not among Christians. This non-Christian residential facility staff "really did save her life," Monica said. "They taught her new things and good things. They taught her how to do things a better way. They taught her that she has value and worth, and things that I just really thought I had shown her. But whether I did or not, she couldn't receive them. So God really loved her through all manner of people."

That's the good news: God is not intimidated or limited by our lack of wits or resources. He will (and does) minister to people with mental illness through the bumbling efforts of church leaders, through the presence of silent companions who keep quiet only because they have no idea what to say, through the efforts of caring people who don't know Christ. When people turn to the church for help, I wish they could always receive accurate and helpful information from caring people who see them as God sees them and not just as people marred by illness. I wish they could receive referrals to a Christian ministry that can help them immediately find the help they need from people who respect their faith and love the Lord themselves. I wish that when they show up at church, they could meet with love and concern that maintains their dignity as people made in God's image.

We may never get there. But if we can take steps in that direction, loving people in Jesus' name, God will honor our efforts as if we were ministering to him (Mt 25:40).

6

MINISTRY LIFE

After writing honestly about, and grieving, the experiences of those who have been hurt and alienated by the church's response to mental illness, I have to acknowledge the legitimacy of the discomfort behind many people's responses. Ministry to people with mental illness has its difficulties. I don't want to pretend that it's no big deal to sit next to someone who's muttering to himself or herself during a worship service. Or that people with mental illness never hurt anyone. Or that it's easy to be in community with a person who needs so much and has very little to give. Or that we should overlook the violations of boundaries, morality and propriety that people with mental illness might exhibit.

Challenges for Church Leaders

Let's acknowledge several kinds of hardship churches face in trying to minister to people with mental illness.

Under the radar. For various reasons, people with mental illness are often reluctant to let others know what they truly need. They may be unwilling to accept their illness, or they may fear rejection or condemnation from the church if they own up to it. They might, like most people, hesitate to ask for help because of pride, discomfort or the sense that they're bothering other people with their problems. Regardless of the reason, if people don't make their needs known, it's usually difficult for other people to help.

I talked with a man who had a career as a pastor, followed by a career in social services. In his experience, struggling people "would keep it a secret until it was too late." The church wouldn't know there was a problem until an explosive event like a suicide attempt got their attention.

A counselor told me about a client with bipolar disorder who told her church what she was struggling with and what she needed. Her church responded, and speaking up was a major growth opportunity for the woman. The counselor said, "She was the type of person who thought, *I can do it all myself* before her most recent manic episode. She was very organized and very on top of things. So to ask for help was just huge for her."

Pastors aren't mind readers, and unless their congregations are tiny, they can't be close enough to everyone to understand the concerns and needs of everyone. So it's understandable that people sometimes fall through the cracks when they aren't open about what's really happening.

Family denial. When mental illness throws families into crisis, some families respond by denying the illness and actively denying their need for help. Even when it's apparent to the church that a problem exists and that the problem may be rooted in mental illness, families might block attempts to help. This may be due to pride—a "we'll handle it within our family" mentality—or a simple unwillingness to accept the illness because of shame or because of fear that the family will fall apart. It's also possible that the entire family system is sick and unable to recognize itself as anything but normal.

One pastor gave me an example of someone who had addiction issues.

The man was severely diabetic, and he was drinking all the time. Even though he was sick, he kept drinking. I asked him to get some help with his drinking. He quit drinking. A few months later, though, they found him dead in his home after he went into a diabetic coma. The house was full of candy. He had simply replaced all the alcohol with candy. The family got mad at me for getting him sober because then the other stuff came out, other issues like depression. He wasn't dealing with things that were going on with him. And nobody wanted to define it. Nobody wanted to talk about it.

The pastor also described trying to help people, or simply to understand what was going on, and "fighting against the tradition of the family, either 'we help our own' or 'blood is thicker than water.'"

In cases like these, the church can do very little to intervene and provide help that people don't want. They can, however, insist on loving people and persistently reach out to them. They can build a loving, accepting atmosphere, free of the stigma. Such an atmosphere would go a long way toward dismantling some of the protective walls families place around themselves.

Spiritual confusion. Earlier I mentioned spiritual misunderstanding and superstition as an issue for people with mental illness. This is also a problem for church leaders. How do you administer spiritual truth to someone who believes she's getting special messages and insights from somewhere else, as my Mom did? She was absolutely convinced she was receiving special insights that led her away from biblical truth. "It was delusions," she said later. "But I thought it was a spiritual gift and the Lord had drawn me close." How could the pastor of Mom's church have known what she was thinking? Should he have tailored his sermons somehow to allow

OF CHURCH LEADERS SURVEYED, 29.9 percent have made special arrangements to accommodate the needs of someone with mental illness.

for this possibility? Of course there's nothing he could have done.

It was the same with the woman I mentioned earlier who was traumatized by her mother's "vision" and graphic accounts of the end of the world. She experiences panic attacks when people talk about conflict between Palestinians and Israel. Her fear has religious overtones that keep her from getting too close to the church.

Some people are traumatized by Christian messages they've misunderstood or mixed with delusions. Such people are unlikely to be open to the church and its teaching ministries. They may respond to acts of love and the fellowship of a loving community, but it's difficult for church leaders to know how to help them understand the truth of God's Word.

Inappropriate behavior. Let's be honest. People with mental illness sometimes behave in ways that make the rest of us uncomfortable. And sometimes they disrupt our activities and communities in ways that should not be overlooked.

I heard a story from a pastor who has a background in social work. She had to call the police when a woman in her church stopped taking her medication and acted out during a service. She was able to get the woman to settle down enough that they could end the service, but then the woman refused to leave the building. "She kept clutching her purse," the pastor said. "And I didn't know what was in the purse." Two men gently asked her to leave, and she hit both of them. "At that point I felt like I needed to call the police, but it was really hard because I had also talked this woman down several times. What frightened me that day was that I couldn't talk her down. Nothing was reasoning with her. So the police came, and they finally took her."

This incident caused real anguish for this pastor. "It was really hard because I really loved her and I cared about her. I had prayed over her, but I had never been afraid before. I had to think about the entire congregation."

Another pastor told a story of a man with schizophrenia

who spent a lot of time walking in the area and often stopped by the church.

> It became problematic. First of all, he stopped by the parsonage where the former youth pastor was living and went into a rant, being verbally abusive and swearing. Then he started stopping by a lot during office hours when we had a nursery school for three- and four-year-olds in the building. The nursery school director was concerned, saying he just couldn't wander around. Other things happened, like a burner was left on downstairs and the back door was propped open, and it might or might not have been Frank, but soon everything was Frank's fault. Everyone started to wonder what Frank might do next, and the trustees decided Frank couldn't be there anymore. I think there were other people who tried to be nice to him, but generally speaking, I think a lot of people were kind of weirded out by him. We didn't quite know what to do with him or where he fit.

Unfortunately, part of the basis for stigmatizing mental illness is the assumption that all people with mental illness will behave inappropriately and unpredictably. This is not true, but I do feel it's important to acknowledge that this sometimes happens. As with any community, unexpected and abnormal behavior in the church can put people on edge and sometimes requires confrontation.

Chaos. Sometimes abnormal behavior goes beyond causing discomfort to actually sowing chaos. Churches can be fragile communities built on formality, and when someone acts on a delusion, a destructive impulse, an unhealthy need for control or a desire for self-harm, the community can shatter or simply fail to hold up under the blow.

A pastor told me about a woman in his church who displayed traits of borderline personality disorder and "created a lot of havoc."

I was always either a hero or a goat, and if I didn't do what she wanted with the children's musical program she would scream at me, "You're the worst person I've ever met in my life." It wasn't just normal human disappointment. She just created a lot of havoc, and people got bent out of shape about it a lot, and she hurt a lot of feelings, but nobody would ever confront her because everybody was afraid of how she was going to fly off the handle this time.

One friend told me about a man who has come to their church several times: "He has a Messiah complex; he thinks he's Jesus.

MORE THAN 40 PERCENT of church leaders have never reached out to and ministered to a family within their congregation with someone who has mental illness; 37.9 percent of respondents became aware of an illness and ignored it, but made sure the person was welcome at church activities. Almost 15 percent (14.7) ignored the person's illness and made no special allowances; 17.2 percent have tried to avoid a person with mental illness until that person was stable.

The first time we saw him he was in the front row doing a very demonstrative dance, and we're not a dancing church. It was disruptive."

After my mom decided she was receiving special insights that led her away from the church, she made the decision to leave the church and announced this decision to my parents' small group. She told them she no longer believed that what they were discussing and learning in church was true. She made a public move out of the church and into the occult. No one knew quite how to respond to this.

Another pastor described a traumatizing event that happened within his congregation. A "quirky guy" complained about something, and a staff member placed that man in leadership over that particular area of ministry. "He drove everyone crazy, drove everyone out of that ministry that he was responsible for." Several months later, this same man confronted the pastor on a Sunday morning over something else that bothered him. "He got very belligerent with me in the lobby of the church," the pastor said. "So much so that another pastor had to come over, and we both had to sort of physically move in his direction in an effort to calm him down and get him away from the general public. And there was some real fear involved in what he might do. So he left the church, and we had some ongoing conversations about how to prevent that type of behavior from happening."

Later, the church received a phone call, telling them there had been an emergency at the man's apartment complex. He had shot and killed the manager of his apartment complex, then killed himself. The pastor said,

> This guy was escalating over a period of time and alienated himself from the church, which made it very difficult for us to respond to his issue. But nonetheless the issue was still there, and had there been an alternative approach, a group or some other place where he could have gone and had some community, I feel like that whole situation could have been averted. I remember getting home that night, sitting on my couch and having a very emotional moment for myself because that could have just as easily been the church lobby as it was the apartment manager's office. I often reflect on that situation and think, *What could we have done to help alleviate that guy's internal pressure that caused him ultimately to take his own life?* I'm perplexed by that still to this day.

Again, I don't want to feed the myth that all people with mental illness are ticking time bombs set to go off at any moment and cause major disruption to the world around them. This is simply not true. In fact, most mental illnesses manifest themselves not in violent acting out but in withdrawal and private suffering. But it is true that some people with mental illness can be highly disruptive and that their behavior affects the community. How do church leaders minister to the whole congregation when these things happen? That question leads me to my next point.

Feeling overwhelmed. For church leaders with Bible college and seminary degrees, mental illness is as much a mystery as it is for lawyers, librarians and lumberjacks. Very few pastors have degrees in counseling or social work, and even fewer happen to be psychiatrists. So when people with mental illness manifest symptoms in the church or come to the church for triage, church leaders may feel inadequate to help.

One pastor, because of her background in social work, knew what to do when a woman at church had a psychotic episode during a service. She and another pastor gently took her home and made sure she was safe. "Some pastors might have just called the police," the pastor said. "But she wasn't harming anybody or putting herself in danger." Would most church leaders know what to do?

One psychologist told me about one of his clients, a pastor, who wanted to discuss a crisis during his counseling session. A woman with a history of mental health issues had come into his office demanding help and behaving inappropriately. The pastor had been forced to respond to the situation on the spot, and he felt completely inadequate to care for her. The situation had overwhelmed him, and he knew he probably would have to interact with the woman again, so he asked this psychologist to give him some feedback and recommendations for next time. The psychologist said, "A lot of people want to care, and yet in some ways feel very inadequate and overwhelmed and often feel guilty and stuck in the process as it plays out, just because of their own sense of not knowing what to do and how to provide that care."

It is important that church leaders without formal training in psychology, counseling or social work acknowledge and accept their limitations. They truly are out of their depth if they're trying to treat mental illness with the skills and knowledge they picked up in hermeneutics class. But making such an acknowledgment of inadequacy is a challenge in itself in a culture that expects our leaders to demonstrate strength, know-how and control at all times. And beyond simply acknowledging their limitations, sometimes church leaders feel truly overwhelmed by the burden of ministry to people outside their expertise and don't know how or when to get the help they themselves need.

Drain. This is perhaps one of the primary difficulties and one of the main reasons church leaders decide not to engage people with mental illness. They suspect getting involved will cost them more of themselves than they can afford to give to one person. And they may be right. Some people with mental illness may demand more of us than they'll ever give back. And the nature of mental illness often means it creates not just one short-term crisis but many crises over the long term, perhaps even over a lifetime.

One pastor told me about "David," a man in his congregation with a history of mental illness, a criminal history and extreme hypochondriasis. He used his hypochondriasis to get attention, and whenever an ambulance drove through town, people joked that David must have called the ambulance for something. Once he called

NEARLY 30 PERCENT (29.7) of church leaders in the survey indicated that when they were aware of mental illness in their congregations, they investigated possible demonic influence and prayed for deliverance.

the ambulance because he felt dehydrated while he was mowing the lawn. He called the ambulance frequently because he had aches and pains and believed something serious was wrong with him.

Another man in the church developed a heart condition and needed a pacemaker. The Sunday after this came to light, David lay down out on a pew during the service and called out that something was wrong with his heart. He was fine, but the church had to treat his concerns seriously.

One day David entered the pastor's office, burst out crying and said, "I'm dying. You'd better start planning my funeral. I have AIDS." When the pastor asked how David knew he had AIDS, he said he had asked his doctor, "Can you tell me for sure I don't have AIDS?" When the doctor said he could never tell him that for sure, David decided the only reason the doctor would say that was because he did have AIDS.

When David sought treatment for an addiction he didn't have, he insisted that the pastor visit him at the treatment center. The pastor didn't visit him, David became upset with him, and their relationship frayed.

"Looking back on it," the pastor said,

I didn't understand mental illness, and I didn't know how to set good boundaries, articulate clear boundaries. I didn't say, "I am not going to come up and visit you during your treatment." I just didn't go, because I was sick of him at that point. He had drained me one too many times. It would have been more helpful if I had been very clear about boundaries, would have been more aware that this was the kind of person who would take everything from me and still not get enough, and still claim that he's under-pastored. So I just gave and gave and gave and then just dropped off, dropped out of his life. Neither one was very healthy. But that's where the giving, giving, giving led.

A senior pastor told me about a staff member who was affected by chronic and profound depression. He wasn't appropriately gifted for his job, and this fed his depression until he stopped doing his job, stopped showing up for work and then couldn't function at all. Because of the church's constitutional requirements, he spent another year in this pastoral role before the church finally gently relieved him of the job while providing him and his family with generous help.

In the meantime, the senior pastor was forced to do both his job and the staff member's job and hear the complaints of people who were unsatisfied with the way the church was addressing the issue. He said,

> It just took a huge toll on me—to the point where I don't think I recovered for a long time. It just gouged me emotionally. Some of it was my responsibility because I made mistakes as a senior pastor. But some of it was just dealing with the mental illness. It was just really, really hard on everybody. Mental illness doesn't just affect that person and his or her family. It affects the whole institution, the whole system.

What this pastor said is especially true if church leaders don't know where or when to draw appropriate boundaries with people affected by mental illness; they may find themselves drained until they're dry.

Church Matters

So why does all this matter? If counselors, social workers and psychiatrists are well equipped to treat people with mental illness and to help them manage and even heal, why is people's experience in the church so important? Because God cares deeply about the sick and marginalized. He judged the people of Israel harshly because "they deprive the poor of justice and deny the rights of the needy among my people. They prey on widows and take advantage of orphans" (Is 10:2). Who is more needy than people suffering from disorders that distort their perceptions of reality itself?

The church matters because Jesus said he came to bring good news to the poor: "He has sent me to proclaim that captives will be released, that the blind will see, that the oppressed will be set free, and that the time of the LORD's favor has come" (Lk 4:18-19). Then he sent out his apostles with instructions to "heal the sick, raise the dead, cure those with leprosy, and cast out demons. Give as freely as you have received!" (Mt 10:8).

The church matters because Jesus said, "God blesses those who are poor and realize their need for him, for the Kingdom of Heaven is theirs" (Mt 5:3). Who is more aware of their daily need for God than the depressed, anxiety ridden, befuddled, lonely and emotionally unstable among us? God sees these people, loves them, calls them to him and calls us to love them.

The church matters because it is the first place many people go when they need help of all kinds, including help with symptoms of mental illness.

And it matters because it represents God and is equipped by the Holy Spirit to pour out Jesus' love on this world. And when someone is rejected, ignored or marginalized by the church—representatives of God—they feel rejected by God.

> **NEARLY 5 PERCENT (4.8 percent)** of church leaders have asked someone with mental illness to leave the church temporarily; 3.2 percent have asked the person to leave the church permanently; 3.4 percent have sought a restraining order against the person.

It also matters because it is a powerful instrument against darkness in the hands of a God who loves the light. The church can and does make a difference. While my family's church didn't really reach out to us, meet our needs, address our questions or assure us it was safe to be the floundering people we were, at the same time our church and youth group were my lifeline. Literally. God used them to keep me from life-ending despair. I never believed God had abandoned me, and the church provided a sane place to grow up spiritually. God used the church powerfully in my life to redeem the challenge of growing up in the shadow of schizophrenia. (For more on this kind of redemption, see chapter nine.)

And I'm not the only one.

My sister Cheryl said, "I felt like church was a haven where I was safe, and that God was my only true comfort. Church and youth group were an escape where we had fun, removed from the weird life at home, and could laugh, think about normal things, feel a part of something good and feel safe since there was no safety at home."

Scott agrees: "My faith has been key for me all through these years of mom's illness. My own personal convictions as well as sermons, Bible studies and theological classes have been very important to give me the strength I needed to live through this experience."

For one girl, the church was literally a lifesaver, providing not only spiritual but also physical sustenance. Church was where she often got food as a child.

When Monica's daughter was in residential treatment, a woman at church told her she and her family were praying for her daughter every day. Their family had a Christmas tradition of drawing a name, keeping it on their table and praying every day for that person. That year they had drawn her daughter's name. This woman had no idea that Monica's daughter was in treatment or even that she wasn't living at home. When Monica shared with her all that was going on, she became a supportive, understanding and kind friend in the church.

Bob Mills was diagnosed with bipolar disorder as an adult and was blessed by his church's response. "Even though I had to recognize that I had an illness," he said, "and that the illness could be treated, I still felt that there was some sort of purpose in all of this. It wasn't just an accident that I got a disease and I'm getting medication and I go see my therapist every once in a while. But I really had a sense that there was something I was supposed to do with it."

Bob often talked with his associate pastor about the situation, and three years after he became stable she asked him to start a support group and community for people with bipolar disorder and their families. The church now ministers regularly to four hundred people through this group, and in eleven years it has reached around 1,500. (For more information on this ministry, see chapter eight.)

A psychologist spoke of clients who have felt embraced by churches and for whom churches have been their primary communities and sources of assistance. Typically this has happened because a small group or a few people, rather than a church body as a whole, have reached out and dealt kindly with their struggling brothers and sisters. The psychologist said, "The theme that tends to come up is connecting with a few people who have accepted them or understood them, or that they felt like they could be with and communicate with. They'll talk about the church they attend, but they really gravitate toward talking about specific individuals or groups who have embraced them as their places of support."

Marlena's father had been shunned by his church. But when he borrowed and wrecked Marlena's car, her church offered her critical support. "Thankfully, I was able to share openly about what I was going through," she said. "I had to. I couldn't survive without the prayer and emotional support I received from my church family and coworkers at the Christian university where I work."

One woman who was diagnosed with bipolar disorder had tremendous support from her church. A counselor worked with her to help her learn how to ask for help and feel okay about it. People would come and sit with her so she wouldn't feel alone when she was in the depressive stage. People would bring her coffee while her husband was at work and help her care for her children, one of whom had special needs. They prayed with and for her and her family. She came to realize she needs help, and it's not just about therapy and medication—it's about the support of the body of believers. Their support has made a lifesaving difference for her and her family.

Stories like these remind me how critical the church's role is in bringing light to the world around us. They also give me hope. There is much the church can do to shine acceptance on and facilitate healthy lives for people with mental illness. Before we get to that, though, I want to take a deeper look at the source that informs the way most of us tend to treat and react to people with mental illness: stigma.

7

PERSISTENT STIGMA

If mental illness and successful treatment are so common in our society, why is mental illness still stigmatized and avoided in the church? Why is it met with wide-eyed panic and awkward avoidance at best? Actually, considering our cultural context, it should be no surprise that people in the church aren't sure how to respond to mental illness.

A Little History

Consider this brief history of the treatment of mental illness in Western civilization. (Incidentally, research and history indicate that mental illness is less stigmatized in Asia and African cultures and in the Muslim world, where people with mental illness have historically been treated more humanely.) In ancient Greece and Rome, people with mental illness were shunned due to a popular belief that their illnesses were caused by evil spirits that might fly out and possess the people around them. Ill people were considered the responsibility of their families, with no hospitals or asylums to house or care for them. If families did not take care of them, people with mental illness might be held in jails or dungeons or allowed to wander the streets.

With the spread of Christianity came a commitment (rooted in the Jewish tradition) to care for the sick. In the fourth century, Christians established the first hospitals and cared for all types of illness, including mental illness. This was in stark contrast to the pagan culture around them, which felt no duty to care for the sick.

One of the first hospitals for treating mental illness was established in Jerusalem in 490, and the church continued to care for people with mental illness. Monasteries cared for some, while the first psychiatric hospital in Europe opened in London in 1247. This hospital, the Priority of St. Mary of Bethlehem, was later given to the city of London, torn down and replaced by Bethlehem, or Bethlem, hospital. This hospital, whose name was often shortened to Bedlam, became famous for cruel and inhumane treatment of its patients. It eventually became a tourist attraction, charging admission of people who came to be entertained by watching the patients. This continued through the 1700s.

Throughout the Middle Ages, people with mental illness tended to be treated better by Christians than they were by the general population. However, the common general belief that mental illness was caused by demon possession led to widespread persecution, including burning and torture alongside those accused of witchcraft.

Through following centuries, the view that mental illness was always caused by demon possession declined, both inside and outside the church. This was due in part to the advocacy of Christian leaders such as St. John of the Cross, Timothy Rogers and Martin Luther, who themselves indicated in their writings that they suffered from common symptoms of depression.

The 1800s brought a wave of asylum reform in Europe. French physician Philippe Pinel pioneered the use of "moral treatment," treating patients with kindness and gentleness rather than torture and abuse. Though authorities were highly skeptical, his methods were, of course, wildly successful. At the same time, devout Quaker William Tuke founded York Retreat in England, establishing humane and compassionate care for people with mental illness. His methods were rooted in the philosophy that people with mental illness were brothers and sisters, capable of living an ordered life. This approach was also successful, and this idea spread and was applied throughout England.

Early in the history of the United States, people with mental illness received care mostly at home. As the country was increasingly urbanized, state governments were forced to recognize and address mental illness as a public issue. States began making provision for people with mental illness within hospitals. The Penn-

SURVEY PARTICIPANTS indicated that their congregations hold to a variety of beliefs about mental illness. These were the most common responses:

- It's a real and treatable/manageable illness caused by genetic, biological or environmental factors, or some combination of the three. (80 percent)

- Like all sickness, it's a painful reality of living in a world poisoned by sin. (66.3 percent)

- Mental illness is a reflection of a spiritual problem that must be treated spiritually. (30.5 percent)

- It's a behavioral problem caused by a person's bad choices. (29.4 percent)

- It's too complex for anyone to fully understand. (21.6 percent)

- It's indicative of demon possession/demonic influence. (19.7 percent)

sylvania Hospital, established in Philadelphia in the mid-1700s, housed people with mental illness in its basement. During this colonial period, most people with mental illness were relegated to jails, almshouses and work houses.

The Quakers brought the idea of moral treatment to the United States, and it was adopted as the presiding approach to psychiatric care. The young nation's first facility exclusively for care of people with mental illness was Friends Hospital in Philadelphia, established in 1813. Other similar facilities were established soon after, all modeled after the York Retreat in England. Clergy were hired to live on the grounds of these hospitals, where they held services and counseled patients in spiritual matters.

Despite the establishment of these hospitals, many mentally ill people, especially those who were poor, were still kept in jails and almshouses, mistreated and untreated. Reformers like Dorothea Dix and Horace Mann advocated for these mistreated people and drove the establishment of many more asylums, intended to administer humane treatment, with the goal of preventing chronic illness by addressing illness early in a kind and controlled environment. Nearly every state in the young nation opened an asylum dedicated to this "moral treatment" approach.

In the mid- and late 1800s, people acknowledged that the moral treatment approach and its early intervention had failed to prevent the development of chronic mental illness, and states built public institutions to house chronic patients. These facilities were overcrowded and underfunded, and because local governments were responsible to pay for treatment in these public facilities, many communities continued to keep their mentally ill citizens in almshouses and jails to avoid the expense. Asylums ran out of money and deteriorated, again providing inhumane conditions.

Around the turn of the century, state governments took over complete responsibility for funding these public asylums, which were renamed mental hospitals. Local governments then transferred anyone and everyone with a mental illness to these state facilities. These hospitals again focused on early treatment and outpatient care in an effort to identify mental illness in its early stages and prevent chronic illness. And again they failed to do so.

Chronic patients filled mental health hospitals, and conditions continued to deteriorate as overcrowding grew during the Depression and World War II. Patients were controlled by the use of medications such as opium, morphine and chloral hydrate. They were treated with experimental drugs and therapies like insulin, Metrazol (a circulatory and respiratory stimulant used in "convulsive therapy"), electroshock, lobotomy and fever therapy (deliberately raising body temperature to cause a fever, sometimes by injecting patients with malaria). One doctor, the medical director of the New Jersey State Hospital, was convinced that mental illness was caused by infections of the teeth, tonsils and intestines. In an effort to prove his theory, he conducted operations on patients in his hospital, removing their teeth, tonsils and other organs and sometimes causing their deaths.

During World War II, people from pacifist religious traditions who were pressed into military service were allowed to serve their country outside the war effort itself as conscientious objectors, some of them working in mental hospitals. They were horrified by the conditions they encountered: decaying and leaking buildings; dramatic overcrowding; people sleeping on the floor; patients with little or no clothing; feces and urine on floors and walls; mixed populations of chronically mentally ill people and elderly senile people living together with children; and staff with criminal backgrounds who regularly beat patients. These Mennonites, Quakers and other people of faith began calling loudly for reform to the system and its abuses.

After World War II came a shift to federal oversight and funding, primarily with the 1946 passage of the National Mental Health Act and the formation of the National Institute of Mental Health. This new era brought another wave of advocacy for early treatment of mental illness and an emphasis on a new concept: community mental health. Armed with new drugs designed to treat psychosis and depression, a new wave of reformers championed the idea that mental health care should focus at the community level rather than the state level, with its large hospitals serving as clearinghouses for people who were "taken away." They drove a massive deinstitution-alization of mental health care, with shorter hospital stays and the release of long-term patients from mental hospitals from the 1950s through 1970. In 1955, state and county psychiatric hospitals housed a total of 559,000 patients. In 1980, that number had dropped to 138,000 as people were released back into local communities.

With federal funding, communities expanded outpatient mental health services, and Medicare and Medicaid began providing limited benefits for mental health care. These benefits spurred nursing homes and general hospitals to open units for mental health care and begin treating patients.

This widespread deinstitutionalization had mixed results at best, theoretically providing a greater number of options for care but burdening unprepared communities, including churches, with the task of caring for people they were not equipped to help and who were largely unwelcome among the rest of the population. Most communities simply did not follow up with creating a system of the kind of care patients required when they were released from state hospitals. Many people with mental illness found themselves in jail, homeless and surviving entirely on public assistance.

Risdon Slate, PhD, is a professor of criminology and chairman of the Department of Sociology and Criminology at Florida Southern College in Lakeland, Florida. He also suffers from bipolar disorder and had his own life-altering run-in with the criminal justice system when he was in need of medication. He said,

The deinstitutionalization movement occurred . . . for all the right reasons. There were some terrible abuses that were taking place in state hospitals. The idea was to move people from state hospitals and link them to treatment in the community. Unfortunately, what has often happened is the linkage to treatment in the community, for whatever reason, has not followed. Where has some of this shift been going? Well, some of it has been going to jails and prisons. The largest inpatient psychiatric facility in the United States is said to be the Los Angeles County Jail. Second largest, Rikers Island jail in New York City. [There are] more people with mental illness in those institutions than in any state hospital in the United States.[1]

Starting in the mid-1970s, a new advocacy movement called for greater community support, viewing people with chronic illness not as hopeless cases but as cases for aggressive and comprehensive treatment. The hope has been to meet people's needs for housing, jobs and other social supports, with the goal of incorporating people with serious mental illness back into community life. New and improved medications and other treatments have helped professionals pursue this goal with some success. People who suffered through mental illness, their families and organizations such as NAMI have developed support networks to facilitate recovery and management and to advocate for policies that benefit suffering people.

ALTHOUGH 80 PERCENT of church leaders said they believe mental illness is "a real, treatable and manageable illness caused by genetic, biological or environmental factors," only 12.5 percent of them said mental illness is openly discussed in a healthy way in their church.

With regard to the existing system for mental health treatment, the US Surgeon General said,

> The de facto mental health system is complex because it has metamorphosed over time under the influence of a wide array of factors, including reform movements and their ideologies, financial incentives based on who would pay for what kind of services, and advances in care and treatment technology. . . . Unfortunately for those individuals with the most complex needs, and who often have the fewest financial resources, the system is fragmented and difficult to use to meet those needs effectively. . . . Many problems remain, including the lack of health insurance by 16 percent of the U.S. population, underinsurance for mental disorders even among those who have health insurance, access barriers to members of many racial and ethnic groups, discrimination, and the stigma about mental illness, which is one of the factors that impedes help-seeking behavior.[2]

In the twentieth century, with the growing influence of Sigmund Freud came an unprecedented separation between psychiatry and religion. With his disrespect and dismissal of religion as "the universal obsessional neurosis of humanity," he drove the removal of religious influence, which he thought to be harmful, from psychiatric treatment. A high percentage of psychiatric practitioners rejected not only the church but belief in God altogether. Until the release of a new edition in 1994, the *Diagnostic and Statistical Manual of Mental Disorders* (DSM) used many religious references as examples illustrating symptoms of serious mental illness.

As we can see with the DSM, the aversion to spiritual issues in psychiatry is changing, with many educational and training programs now including training in religious and spiritual issues and their relationship to mental health. A majority of psychiatric professionals now report personal belief in God and practice of religion. And Christian mental health professionals treat patients specifically from a Christian perspective.[3]

Cultural Stigma

Throughout history, mental illness has met with confusion, misunderstanding and mistreatment—even horror, persecution and torture. Though we have made progress in fits and starts, people with mental illness have never had more hope for productive life than they have now. But despite the progress, we live in a society that is still deeply confused about mental illness.

Have you ever paid attention to the way people with mental illness are portrayed in popular media? While some works, especially more recent ones, treat mental illness with honesty and sensitivity, most of popular media treats the mentally ill as either frightening or funny or both. Most people don't seem to give it a second thought, but for people whose loved ones suffer from ongoing serious mental illness, such portrayals are hard to ignore.

Try watching movies like *Psycho*, *Strange Brew*, *Crazy People*, *The Shining*, *Misery* and *Fatal Attraction* through the eyes of someone who struggles with mental illness. Or turn on the TV this week and watch with a new perspective. On any given evening, you should be able to find at least one show that either reinforces terror of the mentally ill or makes light of their illness for a cheap laugh. News media often mention undefined "history of mental health treatment" in sensational crime stories. Even amusement parks use mental illness to entertain and terrify, with rides like "Psycho Path," "Psycho House," "Psycho Drome," "Dr. D. Mented's Asylum for the Criminally Insane" and "The Edge of Madness: Still Crazy."

The Chicago-area Robert Morris University dance team was criticized for a performance in which they dressed in straitjackets, teased their hair and surrounded their eyes with heavy black makeup. In a *Vs.* magazine photo spread meant to evoke impressions of a psychiatric hospital stay, actress Eva Mendes posed next to the headline "We Are All Crazy for Eva." Burger King received national media attention (and stopped running the commercial) for its TV commercial depicting an "insane" version of their king mascot running from men in white coats and being restrained. A California donut shop, Psycho Donuts, removed its "Massive Head Trauma" donut from their menu after complaints that veterans returning from war would be offended by the donut decorated to look like a man with jelly oozing out of the side of his head. But the shop still features staff in hospital uniforms and a "Psycho Padded Cell" where customers can have their picture taken. Examples abound in popular culture—and they keep on coming.

In everyday conversation, we stigmatize mental illness by casually calling people "crazy" and "psycho." The mentally ill are widely believed to be more violent than the general population, even though studies have shown that this is not true. As with the general population, substance abuse does increase tendencies toward violence, but mental illness itself does not make people significantly more prone to violence than the rest of us. In fact, according to the US Surgeon General, "there is very little risk of violence or harm to a stranger from casual contact with an individual who has a mental disorder. . . . [T]he overall contribution of mental disorders to the total level of violence in society is exceptionally small."[4]

Misinformation, as well as entertainment that pokes fun at people with mental illness—and in some cases encourages laughter at the idea of their mistreatment—accomplishes three things: It further marginalizes and dehumanizes people with mental illness by treating them as caricatures; it's easy to laugh if we forget that we're laughing at real people suffering from real illnesses. It encourages persecution and mistreatment. And it discourages people from seeking help for mental illness. In an environment that vacillates between mockery and horror, who wants to be the one to raise a hand and say, "Yeah, that's me. I need to go to the doctor to get my medication adjusted."

In her book *Darkness Is My Only Companion: A Christian Response to Mental Illness*, Kathryn Greene-McCreight addresses the stigma:

> The worst thing about mental illness, besides the pain, is this very stigma. The taking pleasure from others' pain. The jokes. Stigma creates a fear on the part of the mentally ill and cycles the fear of those who are healthy against those who are ill. I was so ill that at times I couldn't move and yet didn't want to tell my boss why I couldn't come in to work. I had supervisors and colleagues, then, whom I never told. I realize now that I should have done so, but at the time I didn't trust them with the news that I had a mental illness—one that would plague me for life. How could I go back to work after revealing that news? . . . One friend, a professor of theology, actually said about another friend who had been through electro-convulsive therapy (ECT), "His career is finished." Obviously I never told her about my own problems.[5]

The US Surgeon General called this stigma "the most formidable obstacle to future progress in the arena of mental illness and health."[6] When people avoid seeking treatment for mental illness,

CHURCH LEADERS WHO HAVE suffered from mental illness are less likely to feel that their church discusses mental illness openly and in a healthy way, with 9.5 percent indicating as such. Among those who have not suffered, 16 percent believe mental illness is openly talked about in a healthy way in their church.

they may unnecessarily suffer debilitation. And society pays the price—estimated at more than 100 billion dollars a year in the United States. This is despite the highly effective treatments available today, some with up to 90 percent effectiveness. As NAMI says, "Stigma erodes confidence that mental disorders are real, treatable health conditions. We have allowed the stigma and a now unwarranted sense of hopelessness to erect attitudinal, structural and financial barriers to effective treatment and recovery. It is time to take these barriers down."[7]

Serious mental illness has mythological status in our culture. No wonder so many people in the church—just like those outside the church—have no idea how to relate to a real person who acknowledges or displays a mental illness.

Stigma in the Church

This general societal misunderstanding of mental illness affects all of us. In fact, in some ways the stigma within the church may be stronger—with additional layers—than it is outside.

One Christian leader who has serious mental illness in his family told me,

> The confusion of the culture is mirrored by the confusion of the church, which is mirrored by the confusion of Christian families. Christian families are wondering, "Who can I go to; who will listen to me? And ideally, who will listen to me with my perspective on life? My perspective that tells me there is a God who loves me, who sent his Son to die for me." Well, that's the church. There are deeper theological issues and doubts that the church needs to obviously step into. But again, they're as confused as those families.

Let's look at some additional factors that contribute to the stigmatization of mental illness within the Christian community.

The illusion of safety. Some Christians simply misunderstand the nature of mental illness and what it means to be a Christian in a world where "all creation is waiting eagerly for that future day . . . when it will join God's children in glorious freedom from death and decay" (Rom 8:19-21). Their expectations don't allow for the possibility that people who follow Jesus can suffer from illnesses that affect the brain. As one friend put it, "People think Christians aren't supposed to get depressed, because they're supposed to be joyful."

Among people who feel that Christian faith inoculates against troubles like mental illness, accepting the truth that faithful Christians within their own congregations are touched by mental illness opens the possibility that they might be vulnerable as well.

Monica described the way some in her church responded to her family:

> If your kid has a mental illness, mine might too, and I just cannot wrap my head around that. That is just far too threatening to me. I can't deal with you, because I'm too threatened by what you've had to deal with.
>
> It's the idea that if I do the right things and play by the rules and do what God tells me to do, seek purity and seek God, I'm safe. And then my kids are safe. That is just not how it's played out. Because we live in a world that's filled with sin and we feel those effects, whether it's our sin or someone else's, or the general fallenness of the world that touches us. Or sometimes it digs deep into us. Our safety feels threatened when those things happen.

A church leader who leads a support-group ministry to people affected by mental illness described his church as "large, resourced and decidedly pain avoidant." He added,

> While great care and effort is taken to organize outreach overseas—and even across town—the closer the pain is to

home, the more threatening. The suffering of folks with severe and persistent mental illness and emotional wounds is likely the most threatening of all *because it impacts most of our families.* Families most typically stay quiet, for fear that disclosure will have a chilling effect on their social status and inclusion.

Angie said, "One of the things I learned from therapy is there is nothing you need to be afraid to talk about, but that's not the faith system that a lot of churches promote." For some churches, it's much easier to ignore or marginalize people with mental illness than to accept the idea that everyone is susceptible to this kind of suffering.

Mistrust of psychology. Many Christians deeply mistrust psychology and even the idea that brains can be sick and require medical intervention. As I mentioned earlier, psychology is stigmatized in a way most other medical practices are not. And unlike most other medical practices, psychology is considered by some Christians as inherently and irredeemably secular.

CHURCH LEADERS WHO HAVE themselves suffered from some form of mental illness tend to believe their churches hold harsher beliefs about mental illness than those who have not suffered. For example, 23 percent of nonsufferers say their church believes mental illness is a behavioral problem caused by a person's bad choices. Among those who have suffered themselves, 34 percent indicated their church holds this belief. Only 1.5 percent of nonsufferers say their church believes mental illness is a punishment from God for sin, while 5 percent of church leaders who have suffered say the same thing.

This reflects a larger mistrust in science which, frankly, is out of step with Scripture. The Bible says that God holds all people accountable for their response to him since "they know the truth about God because he has made it obvious to them. For ever since the world was created, people have seen the earth and sky. Through everything God made, they can clearly see his invisible qualities—his eternal power and divine nature. So they have no excuse for not knowing God" (Rom 1:19-20). The created world reveals God. How could it not?

This general revelation—and not your testimony or mine—is the primary reason people are held accountable for their response to God. It's powerful and attributable to the work of God alone, and it's one of the reasons destruction of the natural world and urbanization without regard for God's creation should be of special concern for all believers. It's also the reason I believe an honest study of the natural world will never lead a person away from God.

Sure, scientists, like the rest of us, don't always draw the right conclusions. And when accompanied by a deep resentment of God and his people, scientific practice can be heavily biased—just as it can be biased when laced with a determination to prove or disprove a foregone conclusion. But that doesn't make science inherently evil, untrustworthy or even secular. The study of God's created world may be among the most sacred of human vocations.

Among the natural world he has made—through which he reveals his own nature—are our own amazing bodies. Our outrageously complex and mysterious minds, which we are only beginning to understand, are included in "everything God made." Our brains—with their "moving" parts, diseases and astounding strength—are one alluring frontier in the quest to explore a world that only gets more complex with each discovery. And Christians never need fear the study of what God has made.

On top of this mistrust of science, psychology gets a second layer of rejection thanks to the heavily secular influences in its twentieth-century formation. As I mentioned in the brief history above, Sigmund Freud and many mental health professionals who followed him had a strong contempt for religious belief and actually believed religious expression was harmful to people. Again, this large-scale rejection of belief is changing rapidly, and Christian mental health professionals certainly find no conflict between their faith and their practice in caring for others. Even secular professionals widely recognize and respect the value of faith in growth and healing.

Some parts of the church actually gave in and bought into the fallacy that faith has no place in healing and in the life of the mind. They went for a reciprocal rejection and claimed that the mind cannot be sick, cannot affect the spirit and does not require healing. Because of psychology's historical mistrust of the church in recent history, in return some Christians deeply mistrust psychology, including those who practice psychology in keeping with biblical truth and faithful living. They claim that a relationship with God should be all that we need to sustain mental and emotional health.

Dwight L. Carlson tackled this question in his excellent book *Why Do Christians Shoot Their Wounded?*

> Most people consider it appropriate to call a roofer when the roof leaks, a plumber when the sink won't drain, or a tow truck when a car won't start. Though God could miraculously solve each of these problems, in most instances he doesn't. It has nothing to do with his ability or his sufficiency for the task. He is able to, but he chooses not to use that means. Rather, his sufficiency enables me to deal with these problems and get whatever help is needed to solve them. There is no question that God is *ultimately* sufficient.[8]

God created the mind and commanded us to love him with all of it. We needn't fear those who fumble and stumble around in their search for truth. Neither studying the mind nor facilitating healing are innately secular pursuits. One might say, in fact, that they are innately sacred. They can be expressions of faith and wonder in the God who created these complex organs—which are still largely beyond our understanding—and who loves us and, in his mercy, uses the healing presence of other people to grant peace to the suffering.

The wrong kind of people. Some churches stigmatize mental illness because they simply don't want "the wrong kind of people" interfering with their vision for their churches. Pastors can be as guilty of this as anyone else—especially pastors who are obsessed with church growth, focused on marketing and branding their churches with the right image, or looking to enjoy ministering only to the people they most identify with. Let's face it: a thriving ministry to people with mental illness is not the easiest or most ego-polishing kind of ministry.

The ironic thing about this desire to attract only the attractive is that it's impossible to keep the wrong kind of people out of your church. If the wrong kind of people are the wounded, unlovely, annoying, underperforming and neurotic, with closets full of skeletons, they're already among you in great numbers. And 25 percent of them are struggling with some form of mental illness. Most of them are too afraid of the stigma to let anyone know—or perhaps to acknowledge it to themselves.

One pastor told me, "Every church is full of broken, wounded and messed-up people; some just are failing to acknowledge it. It's inauthentic. It causes a schism between reality and Christianity. Scripture tells us to carry each other's burdens. It doesn't say, 'except when you have mental illness or when the person's a little weird.' It just says to carry each other's burdens. We all need help; we all need our burdens carried from time to time. And if the church isn't doing that, who else is going to?"

Any church that demands health, attractiveness and high

performance from its members will succeed in filling itself with people who are good at pretending to be healthy, attractive high performers at all times, regardless of the true story unfolding in the places only God can see. Jesus' term for such people was "whitewashed tombs," which are "beautiful on the outside but filled on the inside with dead people's bones and all sorts of impurity" (Mt 23:27).

This same pastor told me,

> To a pastor who has a fear of acknowledging brokenness and being accepting, I would say, "You need to step aside and let someone rise up within your body who isn't afraid of that because that's not biblical and it shouldn't be a part of church." There is a legitimate fear that acknowledges when we are ill equipped to handle a problem and we may do more damage. But once you have discovered that problem, every day that you don't deal with that, you're negligent.

Something is deeply wrong with a perspective of the church that welcomes only the attractive, desirable and like-minded. A quick glance at the contrast to Jesus' ministry on earth should be enough to convince us that we are not here to be as comfortable as possible. We are not here for the sake of our own achievement, success or happiness. We are here to fulfill the wishes of the one who bought our lives with his own. Who reached out to the least desirable people he could find. Who touched the untouchable. Who said, "Healthy people don't need a doctor—sick people do. I have come to call not those who think they are righteous, but those who know they are sinners" (Mk 2:17).

Social disruption. Unlike society in general, the church is designed as a community of like-minded people drawn together in love and by the Spirit. Even in the presence of the Holy Spirit, the ideal Christian community is difficult to form and sustain among creatures like us, who are consistently bent on our own sabotage.

Because it's full of imperfect and sinful people, the community in churches often feels fragile and finds itself sustained by polite behavior and exaggerated piety. Although we always aspire for better, this is sometimes the best we can do.

In such an environment, people with mental illness sometimes upset the balance and intimidate the rest of the community with unpredictable and socially unacceptable behavior. And while people might show patience with a short-term difficulty, the prospect of ongoing interaction with someone suffering from a chronic mental illness may be more than most people feel they can endure.

Pastors themselves can be put off by the ongoing nature of a chronic illness. According to a post on the website of Pathways to Promise, a resource for those ministering to people with mental illness,

> Sometimes clergy distance themselves from people with mental illness because they realize the problem can be long term. To become involved with this person may mean a lengthy commitment. Perhaps this person will never be cured. Such a problem is contrary to contemporary Western ideas of being in control of one's life and destiny. People in modern day America expect to find a rational solution to any problem. And yet, in this case, there may be no solution. It is tempting, if an answer is not apparent, to avoid the person for whom one has no answers.[9]

Sometimes social discomfort flares into raging chaos. Even in the healthiest and most deeply committed of communities, chaos is difficult and sometimes impossible to accommodate. The church should not be a place of chaos. It is understandable that people don't know how to handle the chaos that mental illness sometimes threatens to introduce. But it's also difficult to know where to draw the boundary, to know what the church should and should not tolerate. So even though the church does not exist for our comfort, many people opt for the easiest solution: tolerating only what they're comfortable with.

The convenience of referral. The increased professionalization of psychology and counseling—even biblical counseling—reinforces pastors' feelings of inadequacy to help the mentally ill and their families. Pastors and others often refer those struggling with mental health to professionals inside or outside the church—and then rest assured that the person's needs are met.

Referral in itself is not a problem. Pastors and others should help suffering people find the skilled and specialized care they need. But in some cases, people are abdicating their responsibility to care for those in their midst, including ill people who are under the care of professionals. As one pastor told me concerning the churches he had served, "One of the assumptions was that we were not equipped to deal with mental illness." People see mental illness as something they're not qualified to deal with, so they ignore it. But when someone is struggling with a different type of physical illness, the church generally doesn't ignore that person, even when they are under a doctor's care.

As I demonstrated earlier, people who are "in the system," especially those who are hospitalized, in jail or feeling their way through medication adjustment, need pastoral care—perhaps more than they did before. Receiving treatment does not substitute for receiving the acceptance and guidance of the church. Psychological care does not meet a person's need for pastoral care and the love of God's people. Treatment may actually bring a new level of spiritual confusion and crisis that makes people more vulnerable to rejection in the church. What a time to abandon a person in need!

Theological challenges. Seeing people suffer with mental illness brings up troubling theological questions many people (or perhaps all of us) would rather avoid. In the decades since I was a teenager, I have heard a total of one sermon specifically about depression—

and no other sermons that even mentioned the reality of mental illness. Several years ago, as I was sorting through some of my own baggage and some theological questions related to my mom's illness, I asked a pastor for help with these theological questions, and he was shocked when I brought them up. He was clearly curious about my story, but as he stared at me, wide-eyed and panic-stricken, I realized he was deeply troubled by my questions and completely unable to help. In fact, I felt as if he couldn't get me out of his office quickly enough because I had caused him to face questions he had tried to avoid. And this was despite the likelihood that through the years he had ministered to hundreds of mentally ill people in his own congregation.

Regardless of our level of education, spiritual maturity and Bible knowledge, and despite millennia of great thinking, we don't have clear and universally applicable Christian answers to these difficult questions. I'm certainly no more equipped to answer these questions than the generations of Christians who have come before me, and a thorough treatment is outside the scope of this book. But I will at least acknowledge a few questions about suffering, accountability, demon possession and punishment.

Suffering. How can a good God allow people to endure the kind of suffering mental illness can produce? How can he allow his followers to suffer psychological terror, anguish and despair? On top of other forms of suffering, some people with mental illness experience spiritual suffering—distortions of truth and torturous thoughts that nurture despair. Why does God allow this? It really boils down to this statement by Gordon Lewis and Bruce Demarest, from their book *Integrative Theology:* "We may suffer in many ways in a temporally limited and fallen world full of conflict with the powers of evil."[10]

I won't attempt to build my own house of cards on millennia of Christian thinking about the problem of suffering. But I will say that the existence of suffering is not at odds with the reality of a great God who loves us and wants us to experience freedom from pain. Someday we will experience that freedom, but until then we live in a world where we should expect trouble. And we should rejoice when that trouble brings us a deeper experience of Christ. Angie said, "When you're broken, you just realize that everybody's got their stuff. It's nothing to be afraid of; in fact, it makes us more dependent on God and able to relate to others. Jesus went through suffering; it's nothing he hasn't experienced before."

Because we often expect less trouble than we encounter in this life, we are tempted to turn away from the kind of suffering that doesn't seem to have an answer. People who suffer through mental illness need us to recognize their suffering with compassion and courage. They need us to affirm the truth that their suffering is like all of ours—a byproduct of imperfection limited to this life, redeemable and not outside the scope of what our faith can live with.

Accountability. Can people with mental illness be held accountable for their choices? Are they responsible for their sin if they are delusional or under compulsion? How lucid is lucid enough to be responsible? And how can God hold mentally ill people accountable for their spiritual choices?

I have wrestled with this question many times over the last twenty years as my mother, who taught me about Jesus and prayed with me when I affirmed my trust in him, waxed and waned in her spiritual understanding, sometimes regressing in maturity and suffering through spiritually charged delusions. These questions tormented me most dramatically when she walked away from the church and Christian practice to embrace the occult. I prayed fervently for her to receive the treatment she needed and more fervently for her to respond to God's grasp and reaffirm her faith.

God gave me the gift of several powerful reminders of his presence with her and his assurance that, while she might walk away from him, he would never abandon her. He reminded me that no one is ever beyond the hope of his reach. I'm thrilled that Mom has come back to the church and now reaffirms her trust in Christ every day. But what if she hadn't? What would that have meant for her eternal destiny? What was the condition of her soul?

I can't answer these questions. I guess this is another one only God can handle. Perhaps the simplest and best approach is to keep reminding ourselves of what Jesus said when he told his disciples how hard it is for a rich person to enter the kingdom of God: "When the disciples heard this, they were greatly astonished and asked, 'Who then can be saved?' Jesus looked at them and said, 'With man this is impossible, but with God all things are possible'" (Mt 19:25-26 NIV).

The work of salvation is God's, and ultimately accountability belongs to him as well. We can always have hope in the work he is doing, unlimited by our limitations and unhampered by our diseases. We may not always know where a person stands, but we are never justified in giving up on anyone.

Demon possession. Is mental illness caused by demon possession? If so, how should it be handled in the church? If not, what role does the person's spiritual condition play in his or her mental health?

Some churches assume all mental illness is caused by demon possession. As Marlena said, "There is a stigma in the church because some people think that all those who are psychotic have demons; they have no room in their thinking for the biochemistry related to mental illness."

Another friend talked about his church's response when he began suffering from panic attacks in graduate school. Determined to rid him of what they saw as obvious spiritual oppression, the church gathered to "pray it out of him." Their prayers didn't cure him, but antianxiety medication has helped him to manage this disorder for years.

Demon possession, even by biblical standards, must be extremely rare. Matthew S. Stanford, in *Grace for the Afflicted*, puts it in biblical perspective:

> We find no reference to demon-possession outside of the Synoptic Gospels (Matthew, Mark, and Luke) and Acts. Exorcism is not mentioned in any of the New Testament letters, suggesting that it may not have been an issue. Many people have wondered if it is even possible for a believer to be demon-possessed. The Scriptures give no examples of demon-possessed believers. . . . In comparison to "natural" illnesses, demonic infirmity and possession are rare in the biblical text and are not even mentioned in a majority of the Scriptures. In addition, we must understand that demon-possession is not possible for those who are "born again," and thus exorcism would not play a significant role in the church either today or in the first century.[11]

So this assumption of demon possession or demonic influence seems out of step with Scripture. Given its rarity in biblical times and the apparent incompatibility of demon possession with new life in Christ, does anyone really believe 25 percent of our population is demon possessed? Automatically asking questions about demon possession distracts us from our calling to minister to people in need. It is harmful and negligent and may discourage a person from receiving critical treatment.

Archibald Hart, a professor of psychology at Fuller Theological Seminary, gives this perspective: "Schizophrenia is a physical disease. Because it exhibits bizarre symptoms, it is frequently labeled as demon possession. But just as we learned with epilepsy (another disease formerly labeled as demon possession), we now know that schizophrenia is the result of a defect in brain chemistry."

Hart provides the following advice, which seems like the simplest and most sensible way to approach a problem that might be mental illness but you also suspect may be symptomatic of demonic influence:

> Consider obvious causes first. . . . For instance, if there is a

history of mental illness in the family and the person you are counseling is experiencing bizarre behavior or emotions, the most likely cause is the familial pattern of illness. Genetic factors strongly influence the severe mental disorders. Unless you are trained in psychopathology, however, the most responsible action you can take is to refer the troubled person to a psychologist or psychiatrist for diagnosis.[12]

Confronting demon possession or demonic influence should not be the starting point for our response to troubled people. If an illness responds to medical intervention, it's a medical problem. And that should be the starting point. If someone displays symptoms of psychological illness, we should not take time to wrestle through questions of demon possession. We should help that person seek and find psychological treatment, walk with the person through the difficult work that will follow and address spiritual issues that linger.

Punishment. Is mental illness God's punishment for sin? Is it a sign that God's judgment has fallen on the suffering person? And if so, how should the church respond?

Monica described some of the blame she felt from people in the church when her daughter was in residential treatment for mental illness:

You're a lenient parent; you let your kids get away with too much. They're possessed; they're dabbling in the occult. Somehow it's their fault or yours. It kind of has to be. But I think we would be foolish to think we know why these things happen. How would I have responded before going through this myself? Probably in very much the same way. I think I would have been compassionate, but my underlying assumption would also have been that they did something wrong.

The question of punishment is complicated because it has two answers: "sort of" and "no." On the one hand, I say "sort of" because all bad things—including mental illness—are consequences of sin in general. We live in a world poisoned by our sin and its consequences, and we reap those consequences every day. In addition, a person's sinful actions and choices can have devastating consequences—and sometimes contribute to a decline in mental health. Consequences are not quite the same as punishment, but close. So "sort of."

On the other hand, the answer is a clear no. In the Bible, both the book of Job and Jesus himself discourage us from seeing illnesses and tragedies as punishment for people's sin. In John 9:1-3, Jesus "saw a man blind from birth. His disciples asked him, 'Rabbi, who sinned, this man or his parents, that he was born blind?' 'Neither this man nor his parents sinned,' said Jesus, 'but this happened so that the works of God might be displayed in him'" (NIV).

Here's another occasion, described in Luke 13:1-5:

> Jesus was informed that Pilate had murdered some people from Galilee as they were offering sacrifices at the Temple. "Do you think those Galileans were worse sinners than all the other people from Galilee?" Jesus asked. "Is that why they suffered? Not at all! And you will perish, too, unless you repent of your sins and turn to God. And what about the eighteen people who died when the tower in Siloam fell on them? Were they the worst sinners in Jerusalem? No, and I tell you again that unless you repent, you will perish, too."

Apparently the people who told Jesus about the temple massacre were judging the victims of the tragedy, assuming they deserved what happened to them. Jesus told them to knock it off and worry about their own sin. Perhaps we should take our cue from Jesus and focus on our own repentance rather than ask questions about punishment and ignore the needs of suffering people while we try to decide whether to blame them for their misery.

Such theological questions can be especially challenging in the face of illnesses like schizophrenia, which are at least largely caused by biological conditions or tendencies present at birth. Such realities are not inconsistent with Christian theology—all creation is groaning under the weight of our sin—but can present a great test of faith. Pastors and other Christians who feel uncomfortable with raising questions they can't easily answer are unlikely to bring them up. And yet people in every congregation must face these questions—with or without the church's guidance. If our theology is too small to allow us to wrestle with them, we need to repent for our lack of faith.

Ultimately it all comes down to this truth, in the words of Monica: "This is a sin-filled world. That's the simple answer. This is a sin-filled world and our minds, our bodies, our brains—they're all affected by that. That's not how God created and intended it to be. I think God grieves deeply when he sees us suffer with these things. He takes no delight. I think his grief is greater than we could even imagine."

Overspiritualization. For some Christians, every problem—and every solution—is spiritual. In this environment, mental illness is obvious evidence of a lack of faith. Medical and psychiatric interventions are suspect, while more prayer and more faith are the prescriptions of choice. While nothing is wrong with more prayer or more faith—mental illness or not—there is not a lot of wisdom in treating illness exclusively with spiritual discipline.

Again, mental illness is called out for special treatment among maladies. A former pastor who now works as a therapist made this point: "I don't hear anybody casting out demons for a heart ailment instead of having bypass surgery. Seldom do you have a pastor saying, 'Well, I can cure that bypass issue with prayer.' With a mental health issue, suddenly we think we can cure that, we can pray that out of a person."

Another pastor and former social worker told me,

Someone asked me the other day, "Do you believe that a person can be healed of mental illness?" I said that's a really hard question. I believe that they can receive healing. I've seen people get better through work and therapy and healing and prayer. I believe God can heal anything. But I don't know exactly how that all works. Can he heal a bad back? Yes, but he might use medicine to heal or to help a person live a better life without all the pain.

Spiritual growth and discipline certainly play a role in healing mental illness and other ailments. One father of a son with bipolar disorder told me,

The heart and soul and mind, they're all integrated. But it's a medical problem, so it's a very difficult thing for a lot of people to understand. It's in the context of interpersonal dynamics that it looks like a spiritual problem. It looks like you could just pray for that person to spend more time in the Word or just pull himself up by the bootstraps and he'll be fine, but that's like telling a diabetic that you'll pray for them when what they really need is insulin.

Another friend struggled with depression when her thyroid stopped functioning properly. Her Christian counselor recognized that she probably had a physiological root to her depression and advised her to see her doctor. Sure enough, she needed medical intervention for her thyroid, and after a long process of working with a doctor, her mood leveled out as her body got what it needed. She's grateful that the counselor sent her to the right place, and she added, "Heaven forbid she would have said, 'Pray harder; you're too weak spiritually; there's some kind of sin in your life that's making this happen.'"

This friend also described the way she sees her ongoing need for counseling:

Long before any of this was a part of our journey, people said, "Therapists shouldn't be necessary. If you pray hard enough and you seek God hard enough, you don't need a counselor." And now, having been in counseling for years myself, I realize a lot of things I wrestle with, they're not spiritual issues as much as they are dysfunction that has been ingrained in me since birth. I need to unlearn those things. So I don't see them as spiritual issues; I don't see them as sin issues. I see them as things I need to learn how to do differently.

When "just have faith and pray more" doesn't work, the mentally ill are shamed and alienated even further. They're also discouraged from seeking treatment, convinced by their churches that their ailments must have a spiritual solution—which remains elusive. This is the work of Pharisees, about whom Jesus said, "Practice and obey whatever they tell you, but don't follow their example. For they don't practice what they teach. They crush people with unbearable religious demands and never lift a finger to ease the burden" (Mt 23:3-4).

This is not the work of Christ, who said, "My yoke is easy to bear, and the burden I give you is light" (Mt 11:30). He does not hold himself out of our reach. He does not hide his peace and demand that we always work just a little harder to find it. He comes to us when we aren't even looking for him, woos us with unconditional love and powers our lives with new strength and supernatural peace each day. He erases the past and gives us hope for the future. He deigns to use us—all riddled with sin and bleeding with shame—in his holy work. He gives us reason to live—the only reason actually worth living for. And all we have to do is come to him like children. May we grant this astounding truth to all suffering people.

I spoke with a NAMI educator whose job is to reach out to her community, helping people understand mental illness and providing the support they need. In nearly a decade of work, she has been discouraged at the lack of participation among churches, which has been a main area of focus for her because of her Christian faith. As she has reached out to churches and offered to help them better minister to people with mental illness within their congregations, most have been uninterested. She described her sadness over

> people within the church, attending Bible study together, staying quiet because of fear. I know that a percentage of them experience depression or other illness, but they don't know that about each other because nobody has decided to share that. If they did, they would probably feel so much comfort. But the church, I think, leans toward that perfection—everything's fine, everything's okay—instead of the real message of Christ: I show you my scars and you're attracted.

In every city in this part of the world, people are working to end the stigmatization and marginalization of people with mental illness. Some of them have received healing or have learned to manage illnesses that affected them so profoundly the world told them their lives were effectively over. Others have seen family members and friends suffer from debilitating disorders and then suffer even more profoundly from the rejection of fellow human beings. Others simply refuse to stand by while people sick with treatable illnesses live in misery or take their own lives because they're too afraid to get help.

Many of them are committed followers of Christ who believe we are all called to behave as Christ did among people in need. Your church can join them in big or small ways. You can start today. How? The next chapter will give you a few examples of churches that are leading the way with ministries especially for people affected by mental illness. It will give you some ideas you can try in your own church.

8

WHAT CHURCHES CAN DO

In this chapter, I'll give specific recommendations for churches. But before I do, let me share some examples of a few churches that are leading by example with intentional ministries to people affected by mental illness.

Start Simple

Menlo Park Presbyterian Church is a large church in Menlo Park, California. Among this church's ministries is the HELP (Hope, Encouragement, Love, Prayer) Mental Health Support Ministry, which meets weekly. Founded in 1999, the group is open to anyone affected by mental illness, both people with illness (copers) and their families and others who support them (supporters). For the first two and a half years, the group was only for loved ones of people with mental illness; when they opened the group to those who themselves were ill, it expanded dramatically and became more dynamic.

Group meetings start with a shared meal and a time of fellowship. This is followed by a program of some kind (such as a discussion or an educational speaker), and then about ten minutes of music and worship. Finally, the group divides into small groups of four who go to separate rooms to share their needs and pray for one another.

After several years, this ministry group decided to host a conference once a year to educate other churches and equip them to minister to people with mental illness. They have since hosted seven or eight annual conferences on mental health. They have felt a calling to encourage other churches to start their own groups and helped about ten churches start similar groups.

About half of the people who attend the group's weekly meetings are from the congregation of Menlo Park Presbyterian Church; the other half are not associated with the church, so this group is reaching out to the community.

Fred and Jane Pramann are in their eighties and have been with the group almost since its beginning. They served as coleaders until their retirement from leadership in 2011, due to age-related health issues and the ongoing needs of their son, who suffers from bipolar disorder and other serious medical conditions. The Pramanns continue to attend the group and are passionate about its ministry and the opportunities they've had to help other churches support people affected by mental illness.

As with so many other compassionate people, the Pramanns' motivation started with their own experience. When their son became seriously ill at age twenty-one, they were shocked and confused by what they were dealing with. They turned to the church "to try to find some help and learn and get some support." Yet they didn't find any. "Our own church, and the other churches that we approached, turned their backs, and we were just left in the cold. There was such a lack of support and understanding and so much stigma that we felt it was important to try to do something about that."

The Pramanns found their way to Menlo Park Presbyterian and a group of like-minded leaders who were affected by mental illness.

"We felt God speaking to us, just calling us to do something." So they joined together and formed the HELP ministry. At first they met twice a month, and "just listened to [others'] stories and prayed for each other, and found that that support was really helpful."

What has made their group effective? The Pramanns claim the most powerful element has been praying for one another in small groups. "People really felt such a tremendous support in that. Prayer has been the big thing that has made the group successful."

They also credit another simple practice: reading their group guidelines at every meeting and asking each person present to affirm commitment to these guidelines each week. Developed by the group's founders, the guidelines state the purpose and expectations of the group. They call for confidentiality, sensitivity and other simple ways of relating to one another that build trust and openness. Repeating these guidelines each week establishes a positive and caring tone for each meeting.

Their most basic advice for anyone who wants to start a similar group: start simple.

AMONG SURVEY RESPONDENTS, 53.2 percent indicated they feel "somewhat equipped" to minister to people suffering from mental illness; 27.7 feel "competent" or "confident"; and 3 percent consider themselves "expert"; 16.1 percent feel "not equipped at all" to minister to people with mental illness.

As the Pramanns answer questions from others interested in starting similar groups, people frequently ask them about disruptions. Fred said, "Everybody's really scared of mental illness and people being on church campus with a mental illness." They soothe people's fears by talking about their own experience. In more than twelve years of ministry, they have had only one group member who presented cause for concern; they asked him to stop coming to the group and to find the appropriate help he needed. They have had no serious incidents. In fact, they say, "Almost exclusively our copers [people with diagnosed mental illness] are a very gentle group of people. Very caring and very loving. It's just a lot of fun being with these folks and having them part of us. All of our married kids are at least eight hundred miles away, and the support group is our family."

This is a grassroots ministry, not highly visible in the church but growing organically among people who become aware of it. "The people of facilities who help set up and take things down, or help out during the meeting, are very much aware, and they are very excited. In fact, one of them said this is the most successful program we have in the whole church."

Thanks to this program, people have come to the church for help and received it. They have found hope. And they have chosen life over death. "We can think of a couple people who have come to us and said, 'Well, if it hadn't been for the group, I wouldn't be alive today; I would have taken my life.' And we've seen people move from being ready to take their lives to more stable and able to go on with their lives in a better way and get jobs, some of them, and so on. It's been a tremendous, valuable program for a church to have."

The Pramanns have benefited as well. According to Jane, "We love doing it. I mean, it just seemed to us such a blessing to see God's hand move in so many people's lives and be able to support them and encourage them. It was so rewarding to us to be able to do it. And we've tried to share that with people, that if they would just give themselves to that type of a ministry it would be such a blessing in their lives."

They echo the refrain of so many humble people who have found themselves surprised and blessed by God's work through them: "We just showed up and God used us."[1]

Delight in Broken People

On the other side of the country, in Winston-Salem, North Carolina, is the Bipolar Support Group ministry of First Presbyterian Church. This group started in 2001 and has ministered to nearly 1,500 people since its inception. Though the ministry focuses on bipolar disorder, some group members suffer with schizophrenia, clinical depression and other disorders. They minister to people with diagnosed illness as well as loved ones. The two groups— people with and without diagnoses—meet separately.

In addition to the support group meetings, this group has worked to educate the church about mental health. They mobilized Christian counselors and a Christian psychiatrist and made presentations to Sunday school classes and men's and women's ministries. They led a two-Sunday program about mental illness and Christianity, answered questions and recommended books and other resources.

The group draws not only people from the church, but also members of the community from all backgrounds—both Christians and non-Christians. Reminders of their biweekly meetings go out to around four hundred people, and their gatherings often welcome people who are returning after five or six years away.

The lead facilitator of this wide-reaching group is Bob Mills, quoted earlier. In his professional life, he serves as associate vice president of advancement at Wake Forest University. Bob is another leader whose ministry flows from his experience. At age forty-eight, he was diagnosed with bipolar disorder after a history of depression and his first manic episode. After his yearlong journey toward stabilization on medication and a few years of wrestling spiritually with what his illness meant for his theology, he was encouraged by one of his pastors to work with his church to start the support group and begin to minister to others affected by serious mental illness.

Bob works closely with local Christian counselors who are

equipped to help people with just about any disorder. He talks about the important role the support group plays: "People want to talk about this stuff. They may not be willing to talk in front of their Sunday school class or their best friends, but they certainly come up to you afterward or send you an email afterward and say, 'We have this problem, and I really would like some help.'"

> CHURCH LEADERS WHO HAVE suffered from a mental illness, such as depression or an anxiety disorder, are more likely to indicate that they are aware of mental illness within their congregations. For example, 96 percent of respondents who have suffered from an anxiety disorder have also seen such disorders within their congregation. Among those who have not suffered themselves, 82 percent have seen anxiety disorders in their congregation. Among church leaders who have suffered from any type of mental illness, 100 percent indicated that they had seen some type of mental illness within their congregation.

When I asked Bob if he had any examples of how this support group has helped people, he asked, "How many hours do you have?" He has tremendous hope, which must be contagious among the people in his group. He says,

> One of the great things is to see people broken. And people don't come to us unless they are pretty darn broken. Even pretty devout folks—they don't really show up unless they are in some considerable pain. And it's wonderful to see the way God will work in that, and then you'll start to sense how they're turning a corner. You can always sense when

they come that this one's going to go very well, and this is the kind of person that may very well become a leader for us, and a facilitator. God just keeps providing in that way.

Bob is passionate about this ministry, humbled by the way God is using him and clear about ministering in Jesus' name.

We make it clear to people that we are there as a ministry, because we believe in Christ and we feel that he wants us to do this, but we want them to come and experience it. And we are there to help in any way that we can. We don't want them to feel surprised that we're going to pray for them and with them if they want, and we're going to be talking about the orthodox Christian view of these things and God's love for them. And people understand that. They do sense that something stronger is going on than what might happen in another kind of support group and that there's a greater degree of openness—that people really do open up and talk.

Bob said he wants other churches to

understand that this is the simplest and cheapest of all ministries because all it takes is broken people who are willing to open up to God and allow him to work through them to heal them and then help them then become healers. It costs the church nothing other than whatever power it takes for us to turn on lights for an extra three hours. And what you get in exchange for that is truly amazing. I mean, it's the depth of healing that people receive. And certainly not just the people who have the illness; the loved ones who come are dealing with tons of stuff, and they're dealing with lots of emotional bondage issues, and pressures that these illnesses bring on relationships are huge. So there's a lot of healing that goes on.

Bob is eager to see more churches openly support people with mental illness. This is his question for all of us: "If one group can serve a thousand people, how many people can a thousand groups serve?"[2]

No One Needs to Feel Alone

Vancouver, Washington, is home to the mental health support group at New Heights Church. New Heights is a multisite church with four locations throughout Vancouver. The mental health support group, which began in 2003, meets at the main campus. The group is designed to provide helpful information, emotional support and spiritual nurturing for people with mental illness and their loved ones. The church has separate support groups for people struggling with issues like depression, anger and chemical and sexual addictions. The church also supports a medical clinic that helps meet the needs of medically and dentally underserved people in the community.

To get started, the group's leaders visited an established mental health support group at a church in another city and participated in its meetings to learn how to start and run their own. They also consulted with a Christian psychologist who advised them on how to facilitate the group effectively. This psychologist continues to consult with the leaders and speak to the group on mental health issues. The group hears from other speakers as well, all of whom volunteer their time (as do the group's leaders). Group meetings usually have about fifteen people. They draw from New Heights Church, other churches and the community.

Elaine Tse and Cindy Hannan started the support group. Cindy is married to the senior pastor, who emphasizes mental health in his own ministry and in his training of other church staff. She developed a burden for people with mental illness after her own experience with depression and anxiety and her son's diagnosis of bipolar disorder. She said, "It was our son's diagnosis and our experiences with him that prompted us to want to start some kind of ministry to families like ours. While we had wonderful support from elders, staff, family and friends, I still felt alone as I knew no one who was dealing with the same circumstances and feelings." Cindy was struggling with her own questions, unsure where to begin, when she met Elaine.

Elaine is a doctor on staff at the church medical clinic, and she is burdened by the silent suffering of so many people with mental illness. When she joined the staff, Cindy found the partner she needed to start the support group.

Elaine and Cindy believe that "with medication, counseling, and good support, people with mental illness can flourish. They also need to be able to find help, home and hope within the church." Their group is helping to provide for people with mental illness within the church.

> People who come to our group find that they are not alone. They learn that mental illness is a common and treatable illness. They learn about their illnesses, living with mental illness, living with family members who are ill, asking for and depending on God's help when mental illness strikes a family of faith. They gain support from group members who have similar experience. All this results in our group members taking the next step toward Christ.

Cindy talks about the ministry the group has had in her life: "Being part of the group helped me tremendously. I no longer felt alone. I had people who understood firsthand what we were going through. I learned a lot from the speakers. I felt loved and cared for by the group members as we shared challenges and prayed for each other."

She feels that this support group has started a healthy conversation about mental illness in the larger church body.

> Mental illness is not an elephant in the room that no one talks about here. It is right out there in the open, just like lots of other challenges people deal with. It communicates that

people with mental illness belong in this church, are welcomed and accepted by this church, and can expect the same love and care and support as others in the church.

Those of us with mental health issues are just like everyone else: broken and in need of a Savior who loves us and will help us. We need the church body to accept us, not be fearful of us, and support us. As more and more people go through this group, I believe the impact will increase.

I asked Elaine and Cindy what advice they would give other churches that want to help people with mental illness and their loved ones. They said it starts with acknowledging that mental illness is common and treatable, and that it strikes both Christians and non-Christians. They also recommended training both pastoral and lay leaders to be aware of and unafraid of mental illnesses: "We all need to know the signs of mental illness, warning signs of a looming crisis and what resources we as a church and community can offer. At the very least, leaders should know what the larger community offers in terms of crisis lines, mental health clinics, NAMI, counselors and social services, so that they can point people in a helpful direction."

> IN GENERAL, CHURCH LEADERS who have suffered from some type of mental illness feel more competent to minister to others who are suffering.

Elaine and Cindy have seen their ministry draw people into closer relationship with God. Elaine says, "People who seek for God's help and depend on him do well, almost always with professional help. They walk closer with our Lord. Therefore mental illness becomes their blessing."

This certainly is true for Cindy:

I have come to the point of being grateful that the Lord chose us to walk the path of mental illness. I know for sure that had I not struggled with depression and anxiety and our son not experienced bipolar disorder, I would never have been prompted to start this group. God allowed us this journey so that he could minister to others through us. He has increased my awareness, sympathy, empathy and compassion. He has graced me with the opportunity to meet some of his other hurting children and exchange hope and encouragement with them. He has loved me through this and given me the opportunity to share that this same love is available to others too. I am so grateful that in our church community there is hope and help and home even for people with mental illnesses. No one needs to feel alone like I did. For that I will always be grateful to God.

To serve as a leader in this church's mental health support group, a person must have a history of mental illness or must have a relative or a friend with a mental illness. Cindy says, "In this way, people who may have at one time been marginalized have a productive place of service for the kingdom of God. We all get to see God use all things for our good (Rom 8:28). For me, that is payday."[3]

Like Nicodemus in the Night

About three hours north, in Seattle, is University Presbyterian Church and its mental health ministry. University Presbyterian is a large church whose motto is "Every Member a Minister." This motto is the basis for formation of groups like the mental health ministry, empowering individuals to exercise their gifts and calling in specific areas. This ministry was founded in 1994 under the umbrella of the church's urban ministry, and it currently serves both people with mental illness and their families. The group's leader has contact with an average of two hundred people a week in the context of this ministry. About 60 percent of participants are connected with University Presbyterian; the rest come from other churches in the area or heard about the group through social service agencies, word of mouth and local NAMI groups.

Weekly meetings are facilitated by the group's leader, David Zucker, and two of the group's participants who serve as cofacilitators. David also hosts eight-week internships for people interested in learning about mental health ministry. He consults with area churches seeking to start mental health ministries of their own. He also collaborates with other churches, parachurch groups, social service organizations and community mental health agencies on strategies for welcoming people with severe and persistent mental illness. David says his most frequent interactions are with case managers in social services who are seeking safe and supportive places for their more spiritually minded clients to get connected.

David works full time on this ministry. After he founded the program, he spent a year volunteering full time, and now he is on the church staff, supported by direct donations to the mental health ministry. Shortly after he became a Christian in his midtwenties, he fell into a deep, clinical depression. The church he attended at the time "initially responded with care, but once they were unable to pray away my agonizing brain disorder, they judged, vilified and all but threw me out on my ear." For several years he avoided seeking mental health care, fully believing his church leaders' claim that psychiatry is anti-Christian.

David eventually found the help he needed, made his way to University Presbyterian and worked as a manager for a faith-based residential community for men and women recovering from serious mental illness. "Our residents were getting better and rejoining the world at an astounding rate," he says. "It was clear to me that the support and accountability of a loving community was the primary reason." When he had the opportunity to start such a ministry at the church, he was enthusiastic.

David is motivated by his own experience, his compassion for others and his awareness of people suffering in silence and shame. When he first started the group, he was disappointed by the lukewarm response among church staff and the congregation. But soon church members began approaching him secretly. He says they were "like Nicodemus in the night, seeking support for their longsuffering family members and themselves. 'Please don't tell anyone here that I spoke with you' became the mantra for these struggling families."

Within a month, his schedule was packed with stealth meetings, mostly off-site, with families in his church. He soon realized the mental health ministry would be reaching into the congregation as much as reaching out. The individuals and families who have themselves been affected by mental illness make the most effective and caring volunteers in David's program. They "get it."

When I asked David for stories of how this group has ministered to people, he responded, "More than I could fit in a dozen books!" (You can read an encouraging story from David in the next chapter.) He pointed out, "A little encouragement goes a long, long way."

His suggestion for other churches is that pastors and other senior leaders support similar efforts in their congregations. "It's a whole lot easier for grassroots movements to get started when they're seeded and watered by folks at the top," he says. "When clergy endorse new ministries, they begin with far more accept-ability and a broader base of participants."

He also has some encouragement for people trying to start such ministries without a lot of support:

The good news is that even in the absence of leadership buy-in, church-based mental health ministries can thrive, provided someone is willing to do the work autonomously, raise their own support and risk taking on some of the stigma of the folks they're supporting. This is certainly not everyone's cup of tea, but I can say, unequivocally, this is the most meaningful and rewarding work I've done in my life. It's exactly what I'd be doing if I won the jackpot in the lottery. How many people can go to work each day and say that? They'll probably have to carry me out of here feet first.

David echoes others in his response to his own suffering and his observation of what grappling with mental illness does for a person:

> So many of us have discovered, in a supportive community, that what doesn't kill you really can make you stronger. Through the years, I've never met an emotionally mature man or woman of God who has *not* traveled through a period of great suffering. With God as our touchstone, suffering builds hope and humility. I've learned that each human being must sooner or later decide if they want to be cool or deep. I'm putting my money on deep.[4]

Recommendations

So if you want to help your church be more faithful and effective in ministering to those with mental illness and overcoming its related stigmas, what do you do? How can churches help, besides referring people to professionals?

A Christian psychologist told me, "People go to a pastor, religious leader, someone in that tradition, before they'll walk into a therapist's office. I've even sent some people. Like when a couple is in crisis and one member of the couple won't come in for therapy, I've asked, 'Is there a pastor or religious leader you would listen to, who could listen to you or meet with you together?' I definitely direct people toward the clergy when it's appropriate."

Ready or not, the church is the first place many people go

when they are in crisis. And if they end up in a counselor's office, sometimes counselors are sending people back to their churches for complementary spiritual and pastoral help. Based on my research, very few churches are ready to offer this kind of help. All of them should be equipped to offer at least some basics. The following pages list several things churches can do, ranked in order from what I perceive as most basic to most complex.

Get help if you're struggling. If you or a member of your family is struggling with your mental health, seek professional help. You cannot effectively minister to a congregation without addressing your own needs. And your first ministry is to the family God has entrusted to your care. Overcome your own fears and prejudices; your suffering or your family member's suffering is not cause for shame. Seek answers to your theological questions. Facing a mental illness doesn't have to destroy your faith. On the contrary, it's more evidence of biblical truth: our fallen world and the creation that groans under the weight of our sin.

Tell your own story. If you or someone you love has struggled with mental health, talk about your experience. Ask God to give you the wisdom you need to discuss it in a way that is healthy, that normalizes the struggle and that communicates grace and solidarity to others. Try to imagine the power of your voice in healing people who feel despised and rejected by the church, marginalized and frightened into silence, wondering if God has turned his back on them.

One pastor told other pastors, "Be vulnerable from the pulpit. Be as vulnerable as you possibly can about your own hang-ups and your own weaknesses. If the lead communicator of God's Word is vulnerable about his or her brokenness, it creates an atmosphere where everybody can be honest about their brokenness." And what is the church if not a place where everyone can be honest about brokenness? What are grace and healing worth if no one needs them?

Get educated. Educate yourself. Unless your congregation consists of mannequins or life-size cardboard cutouts, you can't afford to be clueless about mental illness. You need to understand the people you're ministering to and the types of problems they might have. It's also important to have a basic understanding of the differences between various types of disorders and some of the indications to watch for. A NAMI educator told me, "I think pastors are much like the police—the number-one type of calls they get are really mental health calls." You need to know when you're probably receiving a mental health call.

Other ways to get educated:

- Read one book that provides an overview of types of mental disorders and illnesses. (You can start with chapter two of this book.)

- Contact your local NAMI chapter and ask about the educational program "In Our Own Voice: Living with Mental Illness."

- Rent the DVD *Shadow Voices: Finding Hope in Mental Illness.*

- Check out some of the other resources I've listed in the "Resources for Ministry to People Affected by Mental Illness" section at the end of this book.

- Walk through the mental health care system with someone in your congregation, and allow your findings to help you give support to others as they navigate the same system.

In the words of Cindy Hannan at New Heights Church, "The truth is that there are people with mental illnesses in every church, whether it is known or not. Jesus came to love and serve everyone. He feared no one. All churches can learn to serve the Lord better in caring for his people."

Destigmatize. Make a determined and intentional effort to rid your church of the stigma and shame associated with mental illness. Talk about it. Acknowledge the struggles of people you've

known—and your own struggle, if applicable. Contact local organizations to see how churches can better support the mentally ill.
And if necessary, repent privately or even publicly for the way your
church has handled mental illness.

One pastor spoke of his church's efforts to erase the stigma:

> It's all symptomatic of the original broken relationship be-
> tween man and God; it's all part of being in a fallen world.
> So in the context of the church, we have the luxury of saying
> everyone is in this camp. We've said, Let's approach this
> with grace and God's love and Scripture, and how this ap-
> plies to where you're at. Wherever you are, there is a place
> for you here; come be a part of this community and feel ac-
> ceptance, maybe for the very first time. Everybody's got
> something going on that they need God's grace and God's
> love to overcome. So come be a part of that and receive that.

Talk about mental illness. When was the last time you mentioned mental illness in a sermon or class? Have you discussed
the tough theological questions that mental illness can raise?
Have you established your church as a community of imperfect
people growing in relationship with a God who is not confused
or threatened by our imperfection? Or does your church inadvertently send the message that it's a place only for the mentally healthy?

In my conversations with them, some pastors talked about the
importance of avoiding labels and keeping secrets to keep from
stigmatizing people in their congregations. While it is important to
honor individuals (and the law) by keeping medical information
private, we can discuss mental illness openly. This kind of healthy
openness is what we need. The hush-hush approach actually reinforces and lends credibility to the stigma by suggesting that mental
illness is something to be ashamed of.

Besides sermons, public prayers are a good place to mention

mental illness. As you're praying for those facing other illnesses and obstacles, why not mention (in general unless you have permission) people struggling with depression, anxiety disorders and other mental illnesses?

Consider hosting a Sunday school class on the topic of mental health from a biblical perspective. One of the church ministries that meant a lot to my parents was an adult class led by a professional counselor.

Make your church a relevant, accepting place for those who struggle with their mental health by talking openly about it. One note of caution: no "crazy" or "psycho" jokes. Making light of mental illness is deeply hurtful and alienating, and it reinforces the stigma and shame associated with mental illness.

As you begin talking and teaching about mental illness, please check your theology and your church's teaching and ask God to give you wisdom in discerning and teaching the truth. We are weak and flawed. Mental illness is not a sign of God's scorn or an indication of a lack of faith. We have hope in Christ. His power is made perfect in our weakness. Please don't give people the distinctly unbiblical impression that they shouldn't suffer as Christians or that more faith or prayer will end their suffering in this life.

Encourage relationships. When I asked my parents what the church has done right in ministering to them, they both focused on the open and genuine relationships they have had with a handful of people in the church. Small groups have been lifelines for them, especially when they have been able to talk openly about their struggles, mention their therapeutic work and relate their experiences to the Bible. They also mentioned how helpful it is when curious people ask questions, learning about their experiences and seeking common ground. Questions about what it's like to be on medication or attend group therapy might seem intrusive, but for my mom, they open the door to genuine conversation with people and provide relief from feelings of isolation. Because these are her everyday experiences, they are easy for her to talk about if someone shows interest.

You don't have to be the only one ministering to the mentally ill in your congregation. My parents' small groups and church friends have prayed for and with them, visited Mom when she was hospitalized, taken Dad out for lunch after church when Mom was away from home and shared their own struggles. Genuine and mutual relationships are irreplaceable. Encourage the ministry of genuine relationships in your church so that when mental health struggles and crises arise, those who are suffering have friends to walk through the suffering with them. You might even point compassionate, mature people in the direction of people who need their friendship. As Monica said, "You can't only love hurting people, but you have to start with loving them."

Ask what you can do to help. This is pretty simple stuff, even cliché, but it takes courage. A person who asks this question must be willing to help if the individual or family expresses a specific need. People in crisis don't always know what they need, but sometimes they do, and they feel as if no one is available or willing. Their needs may not be any different from those of others in crisis. If you make yourself available—organize meal delivery, visit someone in a psychiatric hospital, find a ride to a medical appointment, provide childcare, get the kids to school—you may be able to help in some very practical ways.

You may not be a mental health professional, but that doesn't mean you can't help. Be especially attentive to the people who are caring for or living with a mentally ill person. They may be better able to communicate what's really going on and what they need. And like anyone who loves and cares for the suffering, they are suffering themselves.

Be present. This sounds simple, and "ministry of presence" might be cliché, but it's powerful. When an individual is struggling with mental illness, and when that person's family is in crisis, the earth can feel as if it has torn loose from its orbit. People need something stable to help them keep their bearings, and they may need you to help them keep their faith.

Earlier I established the daunting obstacles the system can present, and even people receiving the best of care probably won't receive actual pastoral, spiritual care from anyone but a church leader or mature Christian friend. Even if you have referred someone to high-quality Christian mental health care, that person will receive tremendous benefit from your presence. One Christian counselor told me,

> The kinds of questions clients ask about faith might have never crossed my mind before. I would hope that pastors and associate pastors would be more interested in how they can minister to that particular group of individuals instead of referring and saying, "Okay, I'm done." Yes, they should refer out, but also meet people on the faith side of their journey and not assume that because they referred them to a Christian counselor, their needs will be met. . . . You know, I don't have a theology degree.

A Christian leader who refuses to abandon a family in crisis may be a powerful symbol of the truth that God has not abandoned them either. Make yourself obviously and consistently available, even if it's not clear what else you can do to help.

Radiate acceptance. Refuse to reject the person or family in crisis. Be the person who represents Christ's tenacious and bold love, refusing to be driven away by what you don't understand. Don't leave just because you can't answer all the questions. Don't wash your hands of a family because you've given them a referral to a mental health professional. Like others in crisis, people affected by mental illness need to know that you care. Try to treat them as you would a person who suffers from arthritis or diabetes. Ask questions: Are you managing your illness? Are you caring for yourself? Is the family healthy? Are your family members caring for themselves? A diagnosis or hospitalization doesn't change who a person is; it just changes your understanding of what someone needs.

A Christian psychologist said,

> A strong modeling of grace, love and acceptance, for a lot of people with mental illness, can be very powerful. A number of them have strong issues around authority, particularly male authority. So if they can get a different model of what that looks like, a strong yet caring leader in that pastoral care tradition could be a very important model as well as just a person to reflect God's love to them in talking with them, in being around them.

If it's difficult for you to show acceptance to someone who thinks and behaves in ways you don't understand, prayerfully confront your fears and prejudices: examine where they come from, ask God to purge you of misconceptions and hatred, and replace them with the kind of love he has for the suffering. Again, educate yourself on mental illness in general and perhaps on a specific illness so you can better understand the struggle and behavior of the person under your spiritual care.

Be patient. As I've mentioned elsewhere in this book, mental illness is not resolved overnight. Much mental illness is never "resolved" but can be managed. For many people, success means learning to function well most of the time despite a formerly debilitating illness. People experimenting with medications under a doctor's care may get weird results. Medications that were working may stop working. Some people may relapse or never get healthy enough that you feel comfortable with them.

Mental illness runs on a spectrum of debilitation and chronicity, just as other physical ailments do. While it might be reasonable to expect someone with a broken arm to stop complaining about the arm a year later, it is not reasonable to expect someone with multiple sclerosis to "get over it." Similarly, a case of postpartum depression might resolve itself with a hospitalization, six months of antidepressants and several visits with a therapist. Schizophrenia is another story.

In my conversations with them, several pastors spoke of ministry to people with mental illness in the context of "recovery ministries." This reflects a problem with expectations. Some people truly recover from mental illness, but others don't and won't, barring miraculous intervention. Such illnesses typically can be managed, but the expectation that they should be dealt with and over is false and alienating to people with chronic problems.

One man put it this way: "I don't think churches can say, 'Well, by next year we'll have this thing solved.' No, you'll never have it solved, so just deal with that right now. It's like saying we'll eradicate sin from our congregation. I don't think so."

Don't hold out for people to get well. Don't require them to make you comfortable with them before you'll minister to them. And don't expect them to get better overnight. Ministry among people with mental illness requires a long-term commitment, just like ministry among those undergoing the process of sanctification.

Help with practical needs. My sister, whose husband received a liver transplant after enduring months of intense radiation and chemotherapy, was overwhelmed at the generosity of Christian people who brought meals, mowed the lawn, shoveled snow, cleaned the house, did the laundry, gave rides to their children and even walked the dog and made sure the little pooch didn't miss her appointments at the pet groomer. There's no way my sister could have handled all these everyday demands without help.

Most churches have a plan for providing meals and other practical assistance to families in need, but many overlook the needs of individuals and families affected by mental illness. Like all people in crisis, those affected by mental illness can benefit from a lot of practical help. When they are in crisis, they need meals. When they are adjusting to new medications, they need rides. In the hospital, they can benefit from short visits. Sometimes they need a quiet place to go or someone quiet to come to them. And they very likely need help covering the expenses of medications, hospitalizations and therapy.

As I mentioned earlier in this book, psychiatric medications commonly cost hundreds or even thousands of dollars every month. Churches should not be surprised when patients don't stay on their meds—they may not be able to afford them. And if churches believe it's in the best interest of the congregation for people to have access to the medications they need, they should put their money where their mouths are. Consider starting a fund to help people pay for what a mental health professional or medical doctor has prescribed, with the approval of deacons or another governing group. Consider assisting with counseling fees and hospital bills as well.

For people who are capable of contributing some work in return for assistance, finding ways they can help the church in return may help them retain their dignity.

And please remember family members whose lives are disrupted by someone else's illness. Monica said, "I saw my younger daughter get completely lost in the shadow of the care that had to be given to her sister. It had to. It was a matter of life and death. But someone could have helped by asking something simple like, "Where does your kid need a ride to? Are there lessons that we can take her to?"

Confer with counselors. In talking with Christian counselors, I have discovered very little evidence that church leaders are collaborating with them, asking questions, getting advice and giving input. Church leaders may not realize how powerful their partnership with a therapist can be—or that such a partnership is possible. When you refer someone to a counselor, it is not only appropriate but also highly beneficial for you to talk with the counselor and discuss strategies for effective ministry to the client.

If you want to speak specifically about the client, the therapist needs a signed consent form from the client, indicating that it's all right to talk with you. The counselor can then tell you what strategies they are discussing in therapy and how you and the church can support those strategies to facilitate the person's mental health in the church setting. This kind of cooperation between the counselor and the church can move a person's healing and management of illness forward exponentially.

If you're unable to get the person's consent to discuss her or his case with the counselor, you can still talk to the counselor and get advice on how to minister to someone in your congregation who is struggling with a particular issue. The counselor won't be able to discuss specific people but can give you advice that you can apply in ministry.

Every counselor I spoke with mentioned a desire for this kind of collaboration. One counselor told me, "Pastors would benefit if when they refer people to a therapist, they would also call and get some directives from the therapist. Even if they don't have a release for that particular client, if the pastor would call and just say, 'Tell me about this kind of issue,' it would be helpful for them because I think they would know better how to deal with people."

An experienced counselor and former pastor told me, "In the thirty years I've been a therapist, I've had only one pastor call me and ask permission to come into a session with a client for whom he was concerned, to give his spiritual support. One in thirty years. Why is that? I would say the pastor really helped. He was very helpful. But I don't find that kind of pastor very often."

One pastor, a former social worker, described the collaborative approach her church uses. For people with mental health issues, the church develops a pastoral care plan to help them stay connected to the church and to enable the church to stay connected with the mental health professional. Anyone on the plan signs a release so the church can talk with the professional. "Then we make sure they're attending church," the pastor said, "and getting the spiritual community they need along with the outside therapist or other help. People usually sign the release because they don't want to feel like they're out there on their own. I've had a great response from the therapeutic community because we give them a copy of the pastoral care plan, and they can see who's the pastor to connect with and involve. And I've had therapists say, 'Wow, I wish more churches would do this.'"

Draw boundaries and stick to them. Just because someone is mentally ill, you don't need to suspend standards of morality, biblical theology or respectful behavior in your church community. Overlooking inappropriate behavior or beliefs is destructive to your congregation, and it does no favors for the mentally ill. Regardless of how they respond to social expectations, mentally ill people do need structure and boundaries to grow in independence, understanding and management of their illness. They need healthy people around them to give them objective feedback and an example of mental health.

Help them pursue and maintain health by insisting on a healthy community around them. Communicate agreed-upon expectations openly and lovingly, and hold to them consistently. This is one way counselors can help you—they can give you advice on appropriate boundaries and how to enforce them with people who have various types of mental health issues.

Encourage small groups. Again, for my parents, small groups have been a source of life-giving relationships and a connection to the church when they haven't felt acceptance within the larger church body.

Monica also said small groups have been important in her maintaining a connection to the church throughout her daughter's self-injury, diagnosis and treatment in residential care. "In small groups you have the opportunity to make a more safe relationship," she said. "And that was vital for me."

Your small groups don't have to be specifically therapeutic, and you don't have to form groups especially for people with mental illness. Nurturing a thriving small-group ministry and inviting people with mental health issues to find a place in safe groups may result in the formation of life-saving relationships. One word of advice: it is best to steer such folks toward groups with leaders who are strong, secure and gentle. It is also wise to make sure such leaders know that you are trusting them with some group members who may require special sensitivity or patience.

Know when you are in over your head. As one Christian counselor said, "Pastors should not fool themselves into thinking they can handle everything." Sometimes you need to call in a professional to either handle an immediate crisis or provide long-term care. If you suspect a person in your congregation is struggling with mental illness, refer him or her to a professional counselor or psychiatrist.

Don't wait for a crisis to find the appropriate referral. Compile and keep a list of trusted professionals and their specialties, and make sure you're covering a wide range of specialties on this list, from depression to eating disorders to bipolar disorder and schizophrenia, so you'll have a relevant referral at your fingertips when someone in your church needs it. Bob Mills says, "What's really needed is something that will get people quickly to what they need and to point to good work that's going on. Looking on the Web, it was our conclusion that it's not easy to find things that are very useful very quickly."

This one is an absolute no-brainer: If someone in your church is in danger or is endangering another person, always call 911. This is not a situation for you or your congregation to handle; it's a situation for the police. Once everyone is safe, you can move to referrals and pastoral care as appropriate.

As I've mentioned earlier, referring someone to a mental health professional does not mean your job is done. Please remember the critical role you play in the lives of the people in your congregation, as a representative of God's kingdom. Continue to minister to people who are in professional care. Remember to extend an offer to talk with the counselor or psychiatrist to discuss ways your church can help support the person's health. If she or he gives consent, your collaboration with mental health professionals would be an amazing demonstration of acceptance and love.

Use resources. Even if you know next to nothing about mental health and the therapeutic system, you have more resources at your disposal than you may realize. Take advantage of them. (See the "Resources for Ministry to People Affected by Mental Illness" section at the end of this book for specific ideas.) Get in touch with your local NAMI chapter. Reach out and build a strong relationship with a local, broad-based counseling practice. If there is a local Christian practice that can serve a broad range of needs—from children to adults, from abuse to eating disorders to depression and personality disorders—form a partnership. If that practice is not Christian, forge a friendship and a partnership with them anyway. You can refer people to this practice and also seek advice when you need it. As long as the therapists respect the role of faith and the church in their clients' lives, you can work closely with them.

Be aware that in addition to therapists, your community probably has more places where you can refer people (or where a counselor might refer them), depending on their needs. For example, NAMI and other organizations (and perhaps your local hospitals) probably sponsor support groups in your area not only for people with mental illness but also for their family members. You might find adult daycare centers that can help free family members to work or fulfill other responsibilities when an adult in the family needs constant care. Partial-care facilities and day treatment programs can offer intensive treatment without inpatient hospital stays (or often as a transition from a hospital stay to life at home). Pharmacists can help watch for drug interactions, explain side effects and answer questions about medications. Vocational rehabilitation services (perhaps sponsored by your state) can help with job placement, sometimes in positions designed specifically as opportunities for people with mental illness.

As you become aware of available resources in your community, consider this advice from one pastor: "Develop a comprehensive understanding of the health and human services programs in your specific area—not just to know what you can offer someone or what you can advise someone toward, but to really know where the holes are in your community. Where the holes are, people are going to come to you for that. So it's better to be aware."

Also consider the resources available within your own church. You don't have to be the one engaged in a lot of intentional hands-on ministry to people with mental illness. All the church programs I highlighted earlier in this chapter were founded and facilitated by people profoundly affected by mental illness—either their own or that of someone in their family. I'm writing this book because of my own experience.

You have such people in your church. Who among them might be ready to share their stories and reach out to others? Or perhaps start a support group similar to the ones at the churches I highlighted? Or pray regularly with other suffering people? Consider challenging someone to do this—someone who has traveled far enough in the journey that he or she can unselfishly minister to others and exemplify healthy living.

Bob encourages church leaders to "pray that God will give you people who have been broken by these illnesses." He also offers this counsel: "There are wonderful people who I really couldn't have as the primary leaders of a group because they're not stable enough all the time. That's why loved ones are a real key, and it really needs to be somebody who feels called to do it. A combination of some people who are pretty stable and others who are less so but want to be involved and can be—that's what we have."

One pastor offered another way to make use of people in the church who have experience with mental illness: "Create an advisory council for your counseling and recovery ministries, so that you don't have only a well-put-together staff member or a person who's never been through therapy; you have a team of people who manage the authenticity and effectiveness of your ministry to people with mental illness."

Fred Pramann, from Menlo Park Presbyterian Church, mentioned the benefits of lay leadership for a group like theirs:

> We asked people, "Do you feel like a first-class citizen out in society?"
>
> "No," they say. "I feel like a second- or third-class citizen."
>
> But inside the group, it was a completely level playing field because Jane and I, Betty Mitchell Powell, and the other leaders were just laypeople. So everybody could feel like a first-class citizen, everybody felt that the group was just a very, very safe place. In fact, pastors who have attended a meeting say, "Well, this is a safe place and there's a level of sharing that there isn't anyplace else in the church. If you really want prayer, come to the mental health group and be prayed for."

They also expressed appreciation for what the ministry opportunity has meant to them. Fred—an accomplished man who attended the United States Naval Academy in Annapolis, Maryland, was second-in-command of a ship, earned a master's degree from California Institute of Technology, then enjoyed a career as a design engineer at Hewlett Packard—said, "This has been the most significant and meaningful part of my life, and I've been very blessed beyond anything that I've been able to do before, professionally." Jane affirms this is true for her as well.

Does someone in your church need an invitation to engage in this kind of significant, life-altering ministry?

Start a support group. If your church is ready to make a deeper commitment to support people affected by mental illness, consider whether you are equipped to start a support group. As I mentioned earlier, your community probably has a variety of resources—including support groups—to help people with mental illness. However, most of those groups are not faith-based and will leave matters of faith out of the discussion. Perhaps your church could fill the gap. Or you might partner with other churches to create a support-group ministry to a larger community.

A support group does not have to offer therapy. In fact, unless a therapist is present to facilitate the group, you should not try to conduct therapy. But that doesn't mean it can't be therapeutic. Give people an opportunity to pray together once a month or once a week and to share their stories. If nothing else, this ministry will alert people that they are not alone within the body of Christ and that the church is a safe place to be sick. This message can have more healing power than you might ever know.

Start a professional counseling ministry. If in looking for resources you determine your area is not well served by a broad-based Christian counseling practice, consider filling that gap with a church-based counseling ministry. You could create an actual counseling center within the walls of your church or elsewhere in your community. Or you could locate Christian counselors with varying specialties who are operating independently throughout the area. Invite them into a network of professionals who refer clients to one another and to whom you and other churches refer people based on their individual areas of expertise. You could offer office space to counselors so they can spend part of their professional time working in your church, where people in your congregation might feel comfortable visiting them. Consider what your church can do to fill a need creatively if one exists.

†

So, if you're like most people and you have been unsure how you can help, besides referring people to professionals, take heart and realize that churches and their leaders can do a lot to help heal and support individuals and families affected by mental illness. It's actually easier than you might have thought. You don't need to feel a burden to "fix" or "treat" people. You can start by being a friend and helping to meet their basic needs. You can work with mental health professionals to support their treatment. And where true healing from illness is elusive or impossible, you can demonstrate the kind of love God has for all of us—the kind that doesn't waver, no matter how hard we are to live with.

A Call to the Church

Dr. Steven Waterhouse wrote, "When evangelicals finally do understand this need, then we will wonder how we ever thought Christianity had so little to contribute in the way of ministry. When silence over mental illness ends, churches will discover families of the mentally ill in their congregations. When we remember that pain often results in a search for God, we will think of families of the mentally ill as a ministry that we can no longer ignore."[5]

I believe Christ is calling his church to a great outpouring of love, overflowing from the bottomless well of living water he has placed within each of his people. I believe he wants that love to reach people with mental illness and lift them in a great wave of healing and hope—right where they are, among those our society considers untouchable, avoidable and justifiably condemned to the fringes.

This is what I hope for:

- That we will repent of our rejection of "the least of these," the very people Jesus said represent him as objects of our ministry.

- That we will refuse to continue living in denial, pretending mental illness is a rare problem to be relegated solely to mental health professionals and best not discussed among churchgoing folk.

- That the church will draw itself out of the shadow of the world around us and dare to treat people affected by mental illness with the same compassion and generosity that Jesus showed the lepers and other outcasts he encountered in his time on earth.

- That God will call a group of healthy, compassionate and talented Christians to form a national parachurch organization that supports churches in their ministries to people affected by mental illness—and that this organization will help churches break the silence and acknowledge the biblical reality that our minds are as vulnerable as our bodies to the effects of a sin-infested world.

- That someday people with mental illness will no longer feel, based on their experience in the church, that God has rejected them—that they are beyond hope or not worth caring about.

- That churches will redirect the resources they spend on improving their images and building their brands toward loving and caring for people—the kind of people Jesus went out of his way to care for: the untouchables.

- That the church and its people will be a lighthouse in the darkness, shining with a purpose, guiding storm-battered travelers to safe harbor among people who have been rescued from the storm.

- That the church will be synonymous with hope in the minds of people who can find hope nowhere else.

- That we will learn to carry one another's burdens in such a way that we make it harder to fall than to keep going.

- That in this self-centered, self-sufficient, self-promoting society of the rugged individualist, Jesus' words would ring true: "Your love for one another will prove to the world that you are my disciples" (Jn 13:35).

9

WHAT GOD DOES

I don't know exactly where we all get our ideas about people with mental illness or why we tend to laugh at them and simultaneously believe they're all dangerous criminals. I don't know why we think our jokes and stereotypes aren't hurting anyone. And I don't know why we believe mental illness is so much rarer than it is, why we tend to deny our own mental and emotional struggles or why some Christians have such a hard time accepting the presence of psychosis in a world they fully acknowledge is systemically and pervasively poisoned by sin and death.

I do know, though, that people with mental illness get a bad rap. And the people who love and care for those with mental illness often feel a shame they can't explain and a terrible burden to keep secret what they most need to share. This doesn't stop at the doors of the church.

I'll be among the first to acknowledge that what an illness like schizophrenia does to a person is not pretty. It's an ugly and heartbreaking reality, and my mother's illness has presented the single greatest test to my personal faith. So I'm not trying to minimize the confusion and revulsion we can feel when dealing with people whose brains give them skewed pictures of reality. But like all suffering people, pretty or not, people with mental illness should find solace and acceptance in the church.

All of creation (including our own bodies) groans under the weight of the consequence of our sin. We are all twisted and foul in our natural, hopeless state. We may be uncomfortable and confused in looking at the manifestation of sin's sickness in mental illness, but perhaps it helps to recognize that we are seeing reflections of ourselves in many ways.

People who suffer from mental illness see distorted images of reality, and of God himself. So do the rest of us: "Now we see things imperfectly, like puzzling reflections in a mirror, but then we will see everything with perfect clarity. All that I know now is partial and incomplete, but then I will know everything completely, just as God now knows me completely" (1 Cor 13:12). Someday this hazy glass will be shattered, and we will all see the truth—the truth about who we are, who God is and what is real.

"Yet what we suffer now is nothing compared to the glory he will reveal to us later. For all creation is waiting eagerly for that future day when God will reveal who his children really are" (Rom 8:18-19). We will see each other as God sees us—and we will love what we see. We will know true joy, untainted by sorrow. Our thoughts and perceptions will no longer be distorted by pain, grief, selfishness, greed, depression, anxiety, psychosis or pride. I can't wait until we see him face to face, in a place where sickness has been banished. I can't wait to worship alongside my mom and so many other daughters and sons of God who will have come through deep and acidic waters to see his face clearly.

We are all in this together, and we all have hope in the current redemptive work of Christ and the future and eternal fulfillment of his promise of life without the burden of sin. As Paul wrote to the Corinthian church, "For our present troubles are small and won't last very long. Yet they produce for us a glory that vastly outweighs them and will last forever! So we don't look at the troubles we can see now; rather, we fix our gaze on things that cannot be seen. For the things we see now will soon be gone, but the things we cannot see will last forever" (2 Cor 4:17-18).

Yet our hope is not only for the future. In his grace, God gives us glimpses of the glory to come. He makes old things new. He transforms dead souls into live wires. He cleans, polishes and repairs what he finds in the garbage. He breaks through darkness and shines light into places we thought it could never reach. He changes people from the inside out, and he infuses our stumbling, bumbling, ridiculous efforts to serve him with effective, graceful revelations of himself that somehow cause ripples in the world around us. Our hope for the present is in Jesus and his work in and through us. Sometimes that work brings healing; sometimes it brings a new and deeper perspective on pain. Sometimes it knocks down prison walls that will never be rebuilt. Regardless, it always redeems.

At my eighth-grade graduation ceremony, I stood up and read Romans 8:28, describing the hope I had for the future: "We know that God causes everything to work together for the good of those who love God and are called according to his purpose for them." I believed it then, but I believe it more deeply and with greater conviction now. And I actually understand a little of what it means. My conviction comes from seeing it happen in the decades since.

What's remarkable about this life is not that we have pain, that we suffer, that life gets so ugly we can't even look at it. The remarkable thing is that we have anything but suffering. That there is a large supply of goodness in this world. That despite our best efforts at self-destruction, grace still shines on us, and the sun rises. That we are surrounded by beauty. That we know how to laugh. That we can laugh and cry at the same time. And—most remarkable—that our suffering and pain themselves become the media for some of God's most beautiful work. It's called redemption, and we overlook it every day. God always does this whether we appreciate it or not. And sometimes we actually do recognize it. We get to see it as it happens.

Let me tell you how we—my family, my friends, people I don't know but admire greatly and I—have seen it not only in spite of, but even *through* mental illness.

Redemption Stories

I've mentioned Monica throughout these chapters. Her daughter struggled with self-injury and borderline personality disorder and desperately wanted to end her life. After intensive therapy, life-saving medication and a year in residential care, she has been back home now for a couple of years and has graduated from high school with a radiant sense of peace and hope that she didn't have before.

She still struggles at times, and the rest of the family continues to try to find their balance again. But Monica sees grace everywhere in their story, saying, "If you're looking for nice, tidy, tied-up little boxes, you'll have to look somewhere else. We are still very much in progress, very much on the journey." But she says, "There is huge redemption and hope just in realizing that I don't have to have the answers, because I can't. I can still rest in knowing I'm not going to have them. I think ours is a story of tremendous grace and severe mercy. I don't have the last page of the book, but I see redemption woven all the way through, even in the darkest days when I swore there was no such thing as redemption. Really didn't even care if there was. It's still there."

Marlena, whose father was diagnosed with bipolar disorder and has yet to be stabilized on medication, has herself struggled with depression. Her siblings endure chronic mild depression with episodes of severe depression. But despite all this, she sees God redeeming and helping them. "Sometimes I think we all could have been drug addicts or alcoholics or prostitutes because of the suffering we endured—driven to use other things to anesthetize our pain. But because of the grace of God, we haven't. So that is the redemption I see—God has taught us how to live whole lives so that we flourish."

My brother-in-law Kevin, who has suffered through major depression since childhood, said, "God's redemptive work? It is so evident. The book of James is my favorite book in the Bible because God tells us that trials and tribulations only make us stronger. God has worked through me to get me through. It sounds very strange to say that. But I would not be where I am today if any of this didn't happen. These trials have made me, me."

A friend talks about the benefits of her own suffering. Her anxiety disorder, which significantly impaired her functioning for three years, is now intermittent. This suffering, she says, "has made me absolutely dependent on God. Somehow in God's great goodness, he has allowed me to move through severe anxiety to the point where I can now speak publicly in front of large groups, I'm comfortable leading small groups (something I couldn't do for years and years), and I have a soft spot for people who struggle with anxiety issues."

Angie believes her suffering has made her more aware of God's presence as well as more responsive to other hurting people. Her adoptive parents both suffered with mental illnesses that profoundly affected the way they related to her. She has her own tendency toward depression and anxiety, and she manages her symptoms with medication and counseling. She says her suffering, both as a child and now, "has caused me to rely on God more than if I had not had to deal with some issues. And I have a heart for people who have experienced that and really want to work on their stuff. I think it's enhanced my ministry."

I spoke with a woman who suffered through a difficult marriage to a man with a personality disorder, who had experienced abuse when he was growing up. Her suffering deepened when her husband died of cancer. "But God really brought me," she says, "and even more so with my husband's death, to a place where I truly am desperate for God, and I'm still depending on him. We can fool ourselves in America that we can really do it on our own and think we have all our eggs in God's basket. But really when we come to the end of ourselves is when God makes himself known."

Sometimes God does his work through small steps that many of us might miss. One pastor told me about a woman who started attending her church. She had a mental illness, had suffered abuse, was bound by fear and anxiety, and at first could not even go near the male pastoral staff. But she slowly became a part of the congregation, and the church supported and loved her gently. She became involved in a small group, and members of the group often stayed after to listen to her. They would walk outside with her to give her the courage she needed to leave the building after meetings. After about a year of this, on Easter Sunday, the church's pastor was amazed to see the hurting woman receive communion from a male pastor.

Another pastor told me about a young woman connected to his church who struggled with mental illness and eventually committed suicide. The pastor, who was trained as a trauma counselor, met her non-Christian parents and provided some immediate counseling for them. He then referred them to professionals who could continue their care. They asked the pastor to officiate the funeral for their daughter. He spoke at the funeral about God's work in the girl's life and read some of what she had written about her hope in Christ. He says, "That not only provided comfort, but began the healing process for the mom and dad because they were able to see that even in the darkness of their daughter's life and in her final days, she had a connection to Christ, a sense of love that she communicated in her writing."

This provided tremendous peace for the grieving parents, who did not have a relationship with Christ. When they understood that she had experienced some peace even in her tremendous darkness, they wondered what Jesus could do in their own lives and how he might change their legacy. They both embraced Christ. Their family has experienced great healing because of the small spark of faith in their suffering daughter.

God sometimes uses our small, faltering, surprisingly meaningful actions to change the people around us. Another pastor told me about a woman who came into his office, sat down and said, "I just want to be here. Please don't ask any questions. Let's just sit here." The pastor sat with her for an hour. "I just sat there. I didn't pray. I did nothing. I just sat with her." Five or six years later, when the pastor had moved on to another church, that woman tracked him down and knocked on his door. She sat down and said, "I have to tell you what it meant to me to have you just sit there with me. So often people think there's something they have to do, but I just needed someone to be with me. I'll never forget you, and I will never forget what you did for me."

This pastor told me, "I'll never forget her, because she taught me that sometimes just being there, just accepting the frailty of the human condition, the life that we all face, is what people need. The silent presence of someone else is affirming and nurturing and can make all the difference."

One girl attended a church-based support group with her father. She had suffered an emotional breakdown after college, and she was suffering from depression so severe that she was almost catatonic. The support group walked through depression and treatment with this girl for two years. After receiving electroconvulsive therapy, she began to break through the depression and work in nondemanding jobs. Eventually she was well enough to attend graduate school, earning a master's degree in social work. She worked hard to stay healthy and got all the help she needed, and she now works as a social worker. She will always have to manage her disease, but God has redeemed her acute suffering and given her a new purpose.

Another young man was suffering from severe psychosis and eventually was diagnosed with a serious mental illness. He attended a church-based support group with his mother but was inconsistent in attendance and eventually spiraled downward into drug abuse and found himself on the street. That's when he hit his low point, sought help at a homeless shelter and realized that was not where he should be. He recommitted his life to Christ and experienced divine healing. He still works with a psychiatrist and takes medication to manage his illness, but he is a new person, functioning beautifully. Thanks to hard work and long-term treatment, he no longer hears voices or suffers under delusions. He is beginning to tell his story for the benefit of others in the support group.

A thirty-something mom has had bipolar disorder since childhood, for as long as she can remember. She spent her preteen and teen years seeking to soothe her pain with alcohol, drugs and sex, until she met Jesus at sixteen. Her illness is the hardest kind of bipolar disorder to treat, but she is determined to manage it and to take care of herself and her children. Her symptoms ebb and flow, but she hangs on to Jesus, and she attends a church support group.

The whole group changes when she's there because she's gone through so much that no matter what anyone else shares, she doesn't try to top them—she knows how to relate. The Holy Spirit takes her bruises and scars, and transforms them into radiant love for the other people in the group. And once they meet her, they're hooked. They figure if she can go through what they're going through and come out the other side with Jesus, maybe they can too.

Another woman suffers terribly with a form of bipolar disorder that causes dysphoric manic episodes—that is, rather than uncontrolled euphoria, her manic episodes cause the opposite: a deep, angry, anxious misery. She has lost almost everything due to her illness. She lives day-to-day on disability and a very-part-time job. She attends a church support group, where she is a solid rock and a prayer warrior for others. Just a little disruption or unexpected change throws everything off in her life, but she depends on the provision of God. Her faith builds the faith of the other people in the support group because they journey with her and see how God provides for her.

A woman who fought her way through anorexia and manages an anxiety disorder saw one of her sons fall apart before he was diagnosed with, and treated for, bipolar disorder. Her son is now stable and functioning well on medication. Through the process of supporting him and working through her own issues, she found tremendous healing in prayer. She has emerged as an advocate and a powerful prayer warrior, and she now comes alongside the mental health support group at her church, praying with others in the room next door during meetings and inviting people from the support group to come in and experience times of personal healing prayer.

A bewildered man called the leader of a church support group, desperately seeking support for his profoundly ill sister, who was about to be released from a psychiatric hospital long before she was ready to function well in the larger world. The group leader met with this man's sister, a remarkably bright woman in her forties, and invited her to visit a journaling group. She'd worked for years as an editor, and she liked the prospect of putting her thoughts and feelings down on paper and sharing them with a group of safe, welcoming people.

Though still quite fragile, she wrote so masterfully, the leader soon asked her to cofacilitate the group. Before long, she proved to be a gifted and astoundingly compassionate leader. Within a year, she was publishing editorials on mental health recovery and serving as a speaker for educational seminars. She returned to graduate school, earned a master's degree in counseling and now works for a community mental health clinic. Although she still struggles with a mental illness, this woman brings hope to hundreds and for a decade has been inspiring others to work toward health and healing.

Twin brothers, both with severe schizophrenia, grew up understanding and supporting each other. They spoke with each other in their own language and developed a speech impediment that limited their ability to communicate with others. When one twin died, his brother's secular counselor encouraged him to attend a mental illness support group at a local church so he could practice his social skills.

When this lonely and grieving man found his way to the support group, he wouldn't look at anyone—he kept his eyes down or shut. He talked, though, and even though the other group members had difficulty understanding his speech, they listened patiently. He became a weekly attender and then started showing up early to help set up tables and prepare. Eventually he became a Christian through this ministry and joined the church. He was transformed. Before he died suddenly of cancer years later, he was able to look people in the face, smile at them and talk to them.

Bob Mills saw God work through his illness in a very straight-forward way. Before he became ill, he joined the church "with my fingers crossed," unable to take the step and cross over into belief. For eight years he was a church member but, in his terms, a "sincere agnostic."

What made the difference for Bob was his depression. The church's associate pastor referred him to a Christian counselor, and through therapy Bob realized that "God had put my shoulders to the mat. There were some things that happened then and made me really reach out and then realize I believed a whole lot more than I thought I did. I gave my life to Christ on the counselor's couch."

Later, when Bob's bipolar disorder was diagnosed, his faith gave him a reason to feel that there was a purpose in his suffering. He says, "It wasn't just an accident that I got a disease and I'm getting medication and I go see my therapist every once in a while. I really had a sense that there was something I was supposed to do with it." He began speaking to medical school classes about how to help people with mental illness find spiritual help.

His pastor encouraged him to start a support group. And in eleven years this ministry has helped close to 1,500 people.

Fred and Jane Pramann, David Zucker and Cindy Hannan can all witness to this same kind of redemption: God took their suffering at the hands of mental illness and turned it into the calling and qualifications to minister to others in Jesus' name. And he has done the same for me.

My Family

Now, to end where I began—with my own family. By God's grace (and I'm not using that term flippantly) and for his glory, my siblings and I are all healthy, productive and living in relationship with Christ. We all can say that God has redeemed our suffering. He has made us stronger, with a kind of strength that only his work through great weakness can produce. He has given us a deeper sense of our dependence on him and his comfort in grief. And he has granted us sensitivity to other broken people we might otherwise have shunned.

Mom is currently doing well, managing her illness and benefiting from the advances made in the latest generation of antipsychotic drugs. She enjoys a strong and growing relationship with Jesus and benefits from the ways her church helps her stay grounded in that relationship.

Dad continues to live as a paragon of faithfulness, both to God and to the woman he committed himself to fifty years ago. This faithfulness has been tested many times throughout those years, and his response to God's faithfulness has held their marriage together. He told me about a decision point, driving home after admitting Mom to a psychiatric hospital: "I knew Ephesians 5:25 told husbands to love their wives as Christ loved the church and gave up his life for her. I loved my wife, and I made the decision again that she was my wife for life. I would not leave her. I was going to walk with her through whatever experience we faced. She needed my love, and I needed her."

My parents have always drawn comfort from Philippians 1:6: "I am certain that God, who began the good work within you, will continue his work until it is finally finished on the day when Christ Jesus returns."

My family's journey is not over, and we don't know where it will take us next. But we do know where it will ultimately take us, thanks to God's tenacious redemption plan. I'm proud of Mom's determination to enjoy life and pursue health despite her struggles. I'm proud that she keeps fighting her way back to her family and her faith when other people might give up. I'm also proud of her enduring commitment to Christ.

Dad's faithfulness and his heart—which is absolutely open to the Holy Spirit's work—have not made him a great success in the eyes of the world. But they have made him a great man, more like Jesus than most people I've met. I have been inspired by his passionate pursuit of ministry in Jesus' name, whether in or out of the pulpit. God's redemptive work has used our family's pain to keep my dad's heart soft and ready to serve, and God uses him in a loving ministry toward people who cross his path.

A Blessing for the Church

There is hope! Let us, the church, proclaim that hope in what we say and do.

May your heart be open.

May you understand your own suffering as an opportunity to witness God's redemption.

May you see the suffering within your church and outside your church's walls and respond with sacrificial compassion.

May God's redemptive work cause the struggles of people in your church to blossom into loving ministry toward the suffering.

May you invest what God has given you in things that will last forever.

"Three things will last forever—faith, hope, and love—and the greatest of these is love" (1 Cor 13:13).

NOTES

CHAPTER 2: MENTAL ILLNESS IS MAINSTREAM

[1] "Statistics," National Institute of Mental Health, accessed September 27, 2012, <http://www.nimh.nih.gov/statistics/1ANYDIS_ADULT.shtml>.

[2] "What Is Mental Illness: Mental Illness Facts," National Alliance on Mental Illness, accessed September 27, 2012, <http://www.nami.org/Content/NavigationMenu/Inform_Yourself/About_Mental_Illness/About_Mental_Illness.htm>.

[3] Ibid.

[4] Duff Wilson, "Side Effects May Include Lawsuits," *New York Times*, October 2, 2010, <http://www.nytimes.com/2010/10/03/business/03psych.html?_r=1&scp=1&sq=anti-psychotic&st=cse>.

[5] "Mental Illness Exacts Heavy Toll, Beginning in Youth," National Institute of Mental Health, press release, June 6, 2005, <http://www.nimh.nih.gov/science-news/2005/mental-illness-exacts-heavy-toll-beginning-in-youth.shtml>.

[6] "Epidemiology of Mental Illness," in *Mental Health: A Report of the Surgeon General*, 1999, <http://www.surgeongeneral.gov/library/mentalhealth/chapter2/sec2_1.html>.

[7] "Heart Disease Facts," Centers for Disease Control and Prevention, last modified March 23, 2012, <http://www.cdc.gov/heartdisease/facts.htm>.

[8] J. R. Pleis, B. W. Ward and J. W. Lucas, *Summary Health Statistics for U.S. Adults: National Health Interview Survey, 2009* (Washington, DC: National Center for Health Statistics, 2010), p. 19, <http://www.cdc.gov/nchs/data/series/sr_10/sr10_249.pdf>.

[9] American Cancer Society, *Cancer Facts & Figures 2011* (Atlanta: American Cancer Society, 2011), p. 1, <http://www.cancer.org/acs/groups/content/@epidemiologysurveilance/documents/document/acspc-029771.pdf>.

[10] Centers for Disease Control and Prevention, *HIV Surveillance Report, 2009*, vol. 21 (February 2011), <http://www.cdc.gov/hiv/topics/surveillance/basic.htm#hivest>.

[11] Ibid.

[12] Centers for Disease Control and Prevention, *National Diabetes Fact Sheet: National Estimates and General Information on Diabetes and Prediabetes in the United States, 2011* (Atlanta: US Department of Health and Human Services, Centers for Disease Control and Prevention, 2011), <http://www.cdc.gov/diabetes/pubs/pdf/ndfs_2011.pdf>.

[13] "Statistics," National Institute of Mental Health, accessed September 27, 2012, <http://www.nimh.nih.gov/statistics/index.shtml>.

[14] Ibid.

[15]Ibid.

[16]"Autism Spectrum Disorders (ASDs)," Centers for Disease Control and Prevention, last modified March 29, 2012, <http://www.cdc.gov/ncbddd/autism/addm.html>.

[17]"What Are Eating Disorders?" National Institute of Mental Health, accessed September 27, 2012, <http://www.nimh.nih.gov/health/publications/eating-disorders/what-are-eating-disorders.shtml>.

[18]"Eating Disorders," Mayo Clinic, February 8, 2012, <http://www.mayoclinic.com/health/eating-disorders/DS00294>.

[19]"Statistics," National Institute of Mental Health, accessed September 27, 2012, <http://www.nimh.nih.gov/statistics/1EAT_ADULT_ANX.shtml>; <http://www.nimh.nih.gov/statistics/1EAT_ADULT_RBUL.shtml>; <http://www.nimh.nih.gov/statistics/1EAT_ADULT_RB.shtml>.

[20]Ibid.

[21]Ibid.

[22]Ibid.

[23]"What Causes Personality Disorders?," American Psychological Association, accessed September 27, 2012, <http://www.apa.org/topics/personality/disorders-causes.aspx>.

[24]"Schizophrenia," World Health Organization, accessed September 27, 2012, <http://www.who.int/mental_health/management/schizophrenia/en/>.

[25]"Statistics," National Institute of Mental Health, accessed September 27, 2012, <http://www.nimh.nih.gov/statistics/1SCHIZ.shtml>.

[26]*Diagnostic and Statistical Manual of Mental Disorders,* 4th ed. (DSM-IV) (Washington, DC: American Psychiatric Association, 1994), pp. 273-315.

[27]All sidebar survey data comes from Leadership Journal survey on mental illness in churches, 2010. Used with permission from *Leadership Journal/Christianity Today.*

[28]Mallory Simon, "SNL's Darrell Hammond Reveals Dark Past of Abuse," CNN, October 25, 2011, <http://www.cnn.com/2011/10/24/showbiz/celebrity-news-gossip/darrell-hammond-abuse/index.html?hpt=hp_c1>.

[29]Dahvi Shira, "Kirsten Dunst: Never Having Depression Is 'Weird,'" *People,* September 24, 2011, <http://www.people.com/people/article/0,,20531399,00.html>.

[30]Lara Salahi, "Catherine Zeta-Jones Sheds Light on Bipolar II Disorder," ABC News, April 14, 2011, <http://abcnews.go.com/Health/BipolarDisorder/catherine-zeta-jones-sheds-light-bipolar-disorder/story?id=13373202>.

[31]"Celebrities Diagnosed with Bipolar Disorder," <www.elementsbehavioral health.com/mental-health/celebrities-bipolar-disorder/>.

[32]Doug Farrar, "Brandon Marshall on Diagnosis: 'I'll Be the Face of BPD,'" Yahoo! Sports, July 31, 2011, <http://sports.yahoo.com/nfl/blog/shutdown_corner/post/brandon-marshall-on-diagnosis-ill-be-the-face-of-bpd?urn=nfl,wp4276>.

[33]Mike Fitzpatrick, "American Idol: Singing Against Stigma," NAMI blog, Feb

ruary 7, 2012, <http://blog.nami.org/2012/02/american-idol-singing-against
-stigma.html>.

[34]Bring change 2 Mind, <http://www.bringchange2mind.org/>.

CHAPTER 3: SUFFERING PEOPLE

[1]Trudy Weiss, "The Way I See It—Our Journey through Mental Illness,"
<http://www.davidkurtweiss.com/the-way-i-see-it>, used with permission.

[2]Margaret J. Brown and Doris Parker Roberts, *Growing Up with a Schizophrenic Mother* (Jefferson, NC: McFarland & Company, 2000), pp. 113-16.

[3]Ibid., p. 125.

[4]David Kurt Weiss, "Still Trying Not to Feel," <http://www.davidkurtweiss
.com/home/category/davids-voice>, used with permission.

[5]Anna Weiss, "A Brother's Keeper," <http://www.davidkurtweiss.com/home/
category/guest-voices>, used with permission.

[6]Trudy Weiss, "The Way I See It."

CHAPTER 4: COPING

[1]*Shadow Voices: Finding Hope in Mental Illness*, DVD, directed by Burton Buller
(Harrisonburg, Va.: Mennonite Media Productions, 2005), <http://www
.shadowvoices.com/>.

[2]*National Hospital Discharge Survey: 2009 Table*, cited in "Mental Health,"
Centers for Disease Control and Prevention FastStats, <http://www.cdc.gov/
nchs/fastats/mental.htm>.

[3]These statistics are taken from a number of sources; however, a nice summary
can be found at "Facts and Figures: The Homeless," NOW on PBS, week of
June 26, 2009, <http://www.pbs.org/now/shows/526/homeless-facts.html>.

[4]Doris J. James and Lauren E. Glaze, "Mental Health Problems of Prison
and Jail Inmates," *Bureau of Justice Statistics Special Report* (Washington,
DC: US Department of Justice, Office of Justice Programs, 2006), <http://
www.nami.org/Template.cfm?Section=Press_September_2006&Template=/
ContentManagement/ContentDisplay.cfm&ContentID=38175>.

[5]Michael J. Fitzpatrick, "Department of Justice Study: Mental Illness of Prison
Inmates Worse Than Past Estimates," National Alliance on Mental Illness,
September 6, 2006, <http://www.nami.org/Content/ContentGroups/Press_
Room1/2006/Press_September_2006/Department_of_Justice_Study_Mental_
Illness_of_Prison_Inmates_Worse_Than_Past_Estimates.htm>.

CHAPTER 5: CHURCH LIFE

[1]Dwight L. Carlson, MD, *Why Do Christians Shoot Their Wounded?: Helping
(Not Hurting) Those with Emotional Difficulties* (Downers Grove, IL: Inter-
Varsity Press, 1994), p. 117.

[2]Kathryn Greene-McCreight, *Darkness Is My Only Companion* (Grand Rapids:
Brazos, 2006), p. 36.

CHAPTER 7: PERSISTENT STIGMA

[1]*Shadow Voices: Finding Hope in Mental Illness*, DVD, directed by Burton Buller (Harrisonburg, VA: Mennonite Media Productions, 2005), <http://www.shadowvoices.com/>.

[2]"Overview of Mental Health Services," in *Mental Health: A Report of the Surgeon General (1999)*, p. 80, <www.surgeongeneral.gov/library/mentalhealth/chapter2/sec7.html>.

[3]Information in this section is synthesized from what I learned in these and other sources: Ibid.; Rosemary Radford Ruether with David Ruether, *Many Forms of Madness: A Family's Struggle with Mental Illness and the Mental Health System* (Minneapolis: Fortress, 2010), pp. 137-62; Harold G. Koenig, MD, *Faith and Mental Health: Religious Resources for Healing* (Philadelphia: Templeton Foundation Press, 2005), pp. 17-39; Ricki Kantrowitz and Alex Cohen, "Lesson Plan Two: A Brief Overview of the Asylum and Deinstitutionalization," *Imagining Robert: Study Guide*, Florentine Films/Hott Productions, 2002, <http://www.florentinefilms.org/imagrob/film/stguide02.html>.

[4]"Overarching Themes: The Roots of Stigma," in *Mental Health: A Report of the Surgeon General* (1999), <http://www.surgeongeneral.gov/library/mental health/chapter1/sec1.html#roots_stigma>.

[5]Kathryn Greene-McCreight, *Darkness Is My Only Companion* (Grand Rapids: Brazos, 2006), p. 62.

[6]"Introduction and Themes: The Roots of Stigma," in *Mental Health: A Report of the Surgeon General* (1999), <http://www.surgeongeneral.gov/library/mental health/chapter1/sec1.html>.

[7]"What Is Mental Illness: Mental Illness Facts," National Alliance on Mental Illness, accessed September 27, 2012, <http://www.nami.org/Content/Navigation Menu/Inform_Yourself/About_Mental_Illness/About_Mental_Illness.htm>.

[8]Dwight L. Carlson, MD, *Why Do Christians Shoot Their Wounded?: Helping (Not Hurting) Those with Emotional Difficulties* (Downers Grove, IL: InterVarsity Press, 1994), p. 35.

[9]"The Pastor's Role," *Pathways to Promise*, 1999, <http://www.pathways2promise.org/family/pastorandperson.htm>.

[10]Gordon R. Lewis and Bruce A. Demarest, *Integrative Theology* (Grand Rapids: Zondervan), p. 118.

[11]Matthew S. Stanford, PhD, *Grace for the Afflicted: A Clinical and Biblical Perspective on Mental Illness* (Downers Grove, IL: InterVarsity Press, 2008), pp. 32, 34.

[12]Archibald D. Hart, "Regeneration, Deliverance, or Therapy?," in *Mastering Pastoral Counseling* (Nashville: Thomas Nelson, 1991), available on Christianity Today Library website, <http://www.ctlibrary.com/lebooks/mastering ministry/masteringcounseling/mstmin03-4.html>.

CHAPTER 8: WHAT CHURCHES CAN DO

[1]You can read more about this program on Menlo Park Presbyterian Church's website: <http://mppc.org/connect/help-mental-health-support>.

[2]For more information about First Presbyterian's program, see their website: <http://www.1stpres.com/Connect/SupportGroups/support.html>.

[3]For more information on New Heights Church's support group, see <http://www.newheights.org/support/groups/mental-health-support/>.

[4]For more information, you can find David through the church website: <http://www.upc.org/ministries/congregationalcare/onetoonecare.aspx#mental>.

[5]Dr. Steven Waterhouse, *Life's Tough Questions* (Amarillo, TX: Westcliff Press, 2005), p. 173.

RESOURCES FOR MINISTRY TO PEOPLE AFFECTED BY MENTAL ILLNESS

Following is a list of some resources for those who need help ministering to people with mental illness or dealing with their own disorders, or who simply want to learn more about mental illness. This list contains both Christian and other resources, representing a variety of perspectives and tones.

Books

Dwight L. Carlson, MD, *Why Do Christians Shoot their Wounded?: Helping (Not Hurting) Those with Emotional Difficulties* (Downers Grove, IL: InterVarsity Press, 1994).

> This book dispenses with the notion that hurting people should be condemned for their pain, and helps equip churches to care for wounded people effectively.

Kathryn Greene-McCreight, *Darkness Is My Only Companion* (Grand Rapids: Brazos, 2006).

> An Episcopal priest and college professor shares her theological perspective and stories from her own experience with bipolar disorder.

John Swinton, *Resurrecting the Person: Friendship and the Care of People with Mental Health Problems* (Nashville: Abingdon, 2000).

> A university professor and former mental health chaplain ex-

plores the importance of friendship as a foundational model for ministry to people with mental illness.

Matthew S. Stanford, PhD, *Grace for the Afflicted: A Clinical and Biblical Perspective on Mental Illness* (Colorado Springs: Biblica, 2008).
This book presents detailed information about various types of disorders, with a biblical perspective on each.

Dr. Steven Waterhouse, *Life's Tough Questions* (Amarillo, TX.: Westcliff Press, 2005).
Pastor Waterhouse provides a theological exploration of mental illness and other difficult issues.

Robert H. Albers, William H. Meller and Steven D. Thurber, eds., *Ministry with Persons with Mental Illness and Their Families* (Minneapolis: Fortress, 2012).
This academic work compiles contributions from psychiatrists and theologians, discussing mental illness from medical, theological and ministry perspectives.

Marcia Lund, *When Your Family Is Living with a Mental Illness* (Minneapolis: Augsburg, 2002).
This small booklet, part of the Difficult Times Series, is a tool church leaders can give to families who need support, referrals to other resources and assurance that they are not alone.

Stewart D. Govig, *In the Shadow of Our Steeples: Pastoral Presence for Families Coping with Mental Illness* (Binghamton, NY: Haworth Pastoral Press, 1999).
This book provides inspiration and instruction for pastors in caring for people affected by mental illness.

Harold G. Koenig, MD, *Faith & Mental Health: Religious Resources for Healing* (Philadelphia: Templeton Foundation Press, 2005).
This book explores the history and research behind the relationship between faith and mental health.

Rosemary Radford Ruether with David Ruether, *Many Forms of Madness: A Family's Struggle with Mental Illness and the Mental Health System* (Minneapolis: Fortress, 2010).

A Berkeley professor discusses the history of treatment for mental illness and describes her family's experience in caring for her son with schizophrenia.

Jean-Claude Larchet, *Mental Disorders and Spiritual Healing: Teachings from the Early Christian East* (Hillsdale, NY: Sophia Perennis, 2005).

Translated from French, this work provides an exploration of ancient Christian theology in relationship to mental illness.

Margaret J. Brown and Doris Parker Roberts, *Growing Up with a Schizophrenic Mother* (Jefferson, NC: McFarland, 2000).

Two psychotherapists share the results of their research among people growing up with schizophrenic mothers and explore the effects of that upbringing on the grown children.

Susan Nathiel, *Daughters of Madness: Growing Up and Older with a Mentally Ill Mother* (Westport, CT: Praeger Publishers, 2007).

This book provides insight into the experiences and struggles of women with mentally ill mothers.

Diagnostic and Statistical Manual of Mental Disorders, Fourth Edition (DSM-IV) (Washington, DC: American Psychiatric Association, 1994).

The current edition of a weighty professional resource, this manual is used by mental health professionals in the United States for reference and diagnosis. A long-anticipated fifth edition, DSM-V, is scheduled to be released in May 2013.

Film

Shadow Voices: Finding Hope in Mental Illness, DVD, directed by Burton Buller (Harrisonburg, VA: Mennonite Media Productions, 2005). <http://www.shadowvoices.com/>

This DVD is available for purchase or rental and features stories of people living with mental illness, as well as interviews with mental health experts and clergy.

The Mental Illness Education Project
<http://www.miepvideos.org/>
This organization produces video projects designed to educate, destigmatize mental illness and advocate for better services.

Websites

Pathways to Promise: Ministry and Mental Illness
<http://www.pathways2promise.org/index.htm>
A website hosted by the Missouri Institute of Mental Health "to promote a caring ministry with people with mental illness and their families."

National Institute of Mental Health
<http://www.nimh.nih.gov/index.shtml>
This US government agency's site is packed with information about mental health and specific mental disorders, mental health research and links to more resources.

Wellness Recovery Action Plan (WRAP)
<http://www.mentalhealthrecovery.com/>
This site is the gateway for people with mental illness to develop a Wellness Recovery Action Plan, a personalized plan that encourages people to take responsibility for their recovery and sustained health.

American Association of Christian Counselors
<http://www.aacc.net/>
This membership association website features a "Find a Christian Counselor" tool to help you find a credentialed Christian counselor in your area.

Organizations

National Alliance on Mental Illness (NAMI)
<http://nami.org/>

"America's largest grassroots mental health organization dedicated to improving the lives of individuals and families affected by mental illness," NAMI provides information, advocacy, support groups, referrals and more. While not a Christian organization, NAMI exists in part to provide the kind of support churches and their leaders need.

Mental Health Ministries
<http://www.mentalhealthministries.net/>

Founded by Susan Gregg-Schroeder, a United Methodist minister who has struggled with depression, this ministry aims to destigmatize mental illness and help churches better care for those affected.

Alcoholics Anonymous
<http://www.aa.org>

Recovery and support groups for people with alcohol addictions.

Narcotics Anonymous
<http://www.na.org>

Recovery and support groups for people with drug addictions.

Anxiety Disorders Association of America
<http://www.adaa.org>

An association providing information, support and advocacy for people affected by anxiety disorders.

Eating Disorders, National Eating Disorders Association
<http://www.nationaleatingdisorders.org>

An association providing support and access to care for individuals and families affected by eating disorders.

ADHD, Children and Adults with Attention Deficit and Hyperactivity Disorder
<http://www.chadd.org>
    A nonprofit organization providing information and support to individuals and families affected by ADHD.

ABOUT THE AUTHOR

Amy Simpson is an editor at Christianity Today and a freelance writer, contributor to many church ministry resources and author of *Diving Deep: Experiencing Jesus Through Spiritual Disciplines* (Group), *Into the Word* (Group) and *In the Word* (NavPress).

Amy grew up a pastor's daughter, and her mother suffered (and continues to suffer) from schizophrenia. Her personal experience with the family crisis, personal suffering and church response surrounding serious and chronic mental illness qualifies her to write on this topic with authority, empathy and hope.

Amy is married to Trevor, a licensed certified professional counselor, and is mom to two girls. They live in Illinois.